Waiting for t

Michael Perham
and
Kenneth Stevenson

Waiting for the Risen Christ

A COMMENTARY ON

*Lent, Holy Week, Easter: Services
and Prayers*

First published in Great Britain 1986
SPCK
Holy Trinity Church
Marylebone Road
London NW1 4DU

British Library Cataloguing in Publication Data

Perham, Michael
   Waiting for the Risen Christ
   1. Church of England——Liturgy   2. Holy week
   services   3. Lenten services
   I. Title   II. Stevenson, Kenneth W.
   264'.03   BX5147.H6

   ISBN 0-281-04206-3

Printed in Great Britain by
Photobooks (Bristol) Limited
Barton Manor, St Philips, Bristol

Contents

Preface

The publication of *Lent, Holy Week, Easter* provides the opportunity for parishes and other church communities in the Church of England, and perhaps beyond it, to rethink their celebrations of some of the high points in the Christian year. This little book is offered to the Church to help in the task of implementing *Lent, Holy Week, Easter*, both by providing more historical background to the new rites and also by giving more help in planning the services to suit local conditions than the short introductions to each day in the service book could provide.

This book is the fruit of collaboration between two authors who have brought contrasting perspectives to bear on the work. One of us was present throughout the Liturgical Commission's work on this project over a period of three years; he has seen it 'from the inside', has studied successive drafts, and is committed to the final product. The other of us has taught in a theological college and, more recently, delivered a series of lectures at the College of the Resurrection, Mirfield, which form the basis of his contribution.

Kenneth Stevenson's hand may be detected behind the early material in each chapter, tracing the tradition and enunciating the principles. He is Chaplain to a large university, where he also teaches liturgy. His concern is with sound scholarship as well as with the meaning of each rite and ceremony. Michael Perham's hand may be detected in the sections on how the services may be used. He is Rector of an urban team ministry of new churches, and has come to the texts with a concern for how they may be used within ordinary Anglican parishes, where all sorts of pastoral and practical questions sometimes seem in tension with liturgical principles.

Of course there is overlap, for those who work in higher

education go to church, and parish clergy study books and think hard. So this guide to *Lent, Holy Week, Easter* is not divided conveniently into quite separate halves. We hope that it will seem a fruitful dialogue between the scholarly and the pastoral. We have made this throughout a joint venture, and individual authorship is of little consequence. The remarkable and encouraging feature is that, starting with our contrasting perspectives and backgrounds, we have been united in our enthusiasm for *Lent, Holy Week, Easter*, and in our high hopes for what it may do for the Church.

August 1985   MICHAEL PERHAM
                                 KENNETH STEVENSON

1 Origins and Principles

Modern Revisions

Holy Week is a point in the liturgical year when, in recent years, Christians of many different traditions have learnt to supplement their normal diets with exotic fare, much of it culled from ancient sources. Roman Catholics actually *began* their great movement of liturgical renewal as far back as 1951, when permission was given for the Easter Vigil to be celebrated on Easter night (rather than Saturday morning). This restoration paved the way for the reforms of the entire Holy Week liturgy which appeared in 1956. Finally, yet more reforms were evident in the 1970 Missal, which appeared after the Second Vatican Council, whose own Constitution on the Sacred Liturgy has a strongly paschal flavour, which emphasizes the Easter character of the people of God, worshipping corporately, and enjoying the riches of him who has called us out of darkness into his own marvellous light (1 Pet. 2.9). Anglicans already knew various unofficial adaptations of the traditional ceremonies, including the liturgy of Lent itself, which in many churches involved some form of 'ashing'. At the Reformation, the Book of Common Prayer took a definite stance over Lent, Holy Week, and Easter; the old medieval services were stripped of their special ceremonies, but the essential character of the whole scheme remained, so that Lent began with a penitential service on Ash Wednesday; the Sunday eucharistic readings of Lent remained virtually unchanged; the Sunday before Easter lost its palm ceremonies but kept its passion theme; the days of Holy Week kept their passion readings also, including Maundy Thursday and Good Friday; and, of course, Easter Day celebrated the resurrection, as the outcome of these solemn days of preparation. The Prayer Book could easily be supplemented with simplified versions of the old ceremonies, which is what makes up many of the suggestions in the Alcuin Club's *Directory of*

Ceremonial II (1930). Other churches adapted less, and adopted more, using the old Roman Missal as a starting-point. But the turmoil of Roman Catholic rethinking of the liturgy had repercussions in her sister-churches as well. The community at Taizé, to take a notable example, surrounded its own Sunday liturgy with a strongly paschal piety, and held a vigil (complete with candles, and the reading of the Sunday gospel) on every Saturday evening; it anticipated many of the reforms made in the new Roman Missal. This ecumenical experiment is still alive, affecting the spirituality of many young people, and introducing them to the Easter liturgy in this way.

In this country, the Joint Liturgical Group produced its own *Holy Week Services* in 1971. These both adapt the old ceremonies (e.g. the Palm procession on Palm Sunday) and include elements from the traditions of the churches represented in the Group (e.g. the Methodist Covenant service on the Tuesday before Easter). They appeared at a time of growing ecumenical cooperation; they included a special service for each day of Holy Week, which can be adapted to many different circumstances (i.e. Eucharist or word-service); and they therefore brought together many different Christian communities at a time in the year when those churches could share a common faith in liturgies that were slightly different. Made up of members of many of the mainstream churches of this country (including Roman Catholic), the JLG's work had a considerable impact, which was sustained when a revised version of its services appeared in 1983. Two peculiarities of its proposals need to be noted here. First, in line with JLG's other ideas for the lectionary, they allow special themes to play a significant role in the services, especially on Monday, Tuesday, and Wednesday. Secondly, at the Easter Vigil, the readings come before the ceremonies of light, rather than after them. Both these proposals are novel, and they had to be examined afresh by the Church of England's Liturgical Commission when it prepared services for these days.

Meanwhile, other provinces of the Anglican Communion produced their own service-books. Notable among these was the American Episcopal Church, whose Book of Common

Prayer (1979) took an adaptive line between previous Anglican tradition (from the Reformation) and present-day ecumenical renewal. Thus, Lent starts with a liturgy which includes elements from the old Prayer Book Commination service and the new Roman Catholic rite of ashing. Palm Sunday keeps its passion gospel but prefixes the (by now popular) palm gospel and procession, before the main Eucharist. Maundy Thursday and Good Friday know similar adaptations. For the Easter Liturgy itself, provision is made for the traditional Vigil, consisting of ceremonies of light, readings, baptism, and Eucharist. But those churches which cannot mount that elaborate service can begin their main Easter morning Eucharist with the ceremonies of light, and include the renewal of baptismal vows after the sermon. Clearly, by the time the Liturgical Commission set about the task of producing services for Lent, Holy Week, and Easter, it had the advantage of being able to take stock of all these new forms of service. And, unlike the contents of the *Alternative Service Book* (1980), these new services did not have to endure the process of Revision Committees of General Synod, since they are supplementary rites, in no way rivalling the legal character of the Prayer Book.

Three pieties?

So much for recent history. What of the pieties which these new services will meet in ordinary congregations? Piety is as slippery as a banana-skin, and to describe it is fraught with problems. But history can, once more, illuminate much of what we have inherited. There are three different approaches to religious experience which have a direct bearing on how people have assimilated what many writers nowadays call 'the Easter mystery'. The first corresponds to the earliest kind of Christian spirituality, which can be described as 'unitive'. There is no evidence for any kind of planned Holy Week in the first three centuries. Christians celebrated the death and resurrection of Christ in one, single liturgy. The old Jewish Passover is replaced by the Christian Passover, which becomes a long, overnight liturgy. Death and resurrection belong together, so they are not

3

separated. Old Testament readings become treated typologically in this liturgy, so that (for example) the people of Israel's escape through the Red Sea is seen as a 'type' of the people of the New Israel's deliverance from sin and death through Christ. By the third century, baptism is increasingly restricted to Easter, so that new Christians can spiritually be reborn when the rest of the Church is celebrating its primal deliverance. Since there was no such thing as Christmas at this time, the impact of an Easter baptism must have been considerable, not only on the new Christians themselves, but on the whole Christian community. It is difficult for us to understand this, both because we live in such a different world, and also because we are heirs of the residue of so much Christian history, liturgical development, and theological controversy. The ancients did it all in one fell swoop, because for them the whole story could be held together, as a unity. It is from this 'unitive' piety that the Easter Vigil is derived, with its fourfold symbolic celebration of the Christian Pasch, in light, word, water, and in bread and wine.

The second piety surfaces in the fourth century, and it is the result of what liturgists have clumsily called 'historicization'. It appears in a charming travel-diary of a nun, called Egeria, who spent several memorable Lents, Holy Weeks, and Easters at Jerusalem in the latter part of the fourth century, probably between 381 and 384. Egeria's home was either France or Spain, at the Atlantic sea-board. What she notes in her diary is exactly what an ordinary travel-diary contains - what is new and different. Her descriptions of the Jerusalem service are clear and concise. She does not suffer from the sacristy mind; she goes straight to the heart of the matter, at every point. (The diary has been edited, with copious notes, by John Wilkinson, and has appeared as *Egeria's Travels* in two editions, one by SPCK, in 1971, and another, with corrections and extra notes, by Aris and Phillips, in 1981.)

The kind of piety which Egeria describes in these Jerusalem liturgies is 'rememorative', because it is at root historical in its approach, and its services are meant to remind the worshippers of certain 'events', in order to build up their religious experience. Jerusalem is an obvious place for such a piety to

4

reach an early stage of development, because all the 'events' of Holy Week and Easter 'happened' in and around that city. Interestingly, Egeria recognizes much of the old Vigil liturgy, but she notes the special treatment of its baptism. We know from other sources that Cyril of Jerusalem emphasized the 'dying and rising with Christ' in baptism (cf. Rom. 6.3-11), which is entirely in accord with what Egeria saw, namely that new Christians were baptized at the place traditionally associated with Christ's burial. The symbolism could not be more direct!

But the really new features which Egeria notices are what make up the historical character of the week. Working backwards from the Easter Vigil baptism and Eucharist, we find the following. Friday celebrates the crucifixion, and a 'relic' of the true cross is held firmly down on a table while the scores of faithful come up to venerate it. Thursday commemorates the Last Supper and betrayal. Wednesday commemorates Judas' pact with the Jewish priests. On the afternoon of the Sunday before, there is a procession down the Mount of Olives. Here are the germs of the later Holy Week. But two features are to be noted. First, the services are all linked together. They read like one long play, made up of many acts and scenes. There is even a slightly relentless feel to the entire week. (Such a wholesome view of the week would be easy to keep in Jerusalem.) Secondly, because the special services are 'rememorative' in their form, drama is kept to a minimum. Thus, the procession on Palm Sunday does not involve anything pictorial; there is no donkey. Similarly, the relic of the cross is venerated, but there is no attempt at a re-enactment (in whatever form) of the crucifixion itself. The 'events' are allowed to speak for themselves, and Scripture is invariably used to interpret them. The message is subtly suggested, not hammered home. The piety is no longer 'unitive' because history and geography have been allowed to take over in order to enrich an older, simpler scheme. The 'events' are called to mind, but are celebrated in liturgy's truest form, a symbolic code.

But another piety creeps in, which turns the 'rememorative' rites which Egeria describes into the 'representational' ones of

5

the later Middle Ages. Thus, the Easter Vigil is interrupted by a mini-drama, in which robed ministers act the parts of the women at the tomb, providing the foundations for the popular *quem queritis* which seems to have made its first appearance in the Anglo-Saxon *Regularis Concordia* in the tenth century. 'Representational' piety is a bid to rescue 'rememorative' rites from their austerity and obliqueness, in an attempt to make the liturgy meaningful and relevant. Thus, the body of Christ is 'buried' in an Easter sepulchre, which was often a special architectural feature of medieval churches. Similarly, the celebrant washes the feet of certain members of the community on Maundy Thursday, a custom which King John took over, thereby establishing a tradition which was secularized into Maundy money and which is still part of the sovereign's annual routine. On Palm Sunday, the palm procession is prefixed to the (older) passion theme mass, and an elaborate rite develops, with readings and blessings, in order to recreate the atmosphere of the first Palm Sunday. Finally, Lent becomes a journey into the wilderness with Christ, instead of a preparation for Easter. Representational liturgy is, by its nature, more vulgar, less subtle than the rememorative, because its world is that of pictures and drama, rather than symbols and codes. The picture is painted, in greater or lesser starkness, and it is presented to the faithful. The earlier symbolic form, by contrast, permits the faithful to relate in different ways and at different levels, because the meaning is never spelt out to them.

At the Reformation, representational piety persisted, even though the rites and ceremonies associated with it were abolished as being superstitious. Both in the Churches of the Reformation which abolished the entire liturgical year (Reformed, Presbyterian, and Independent) and also in those which kept it (Lutheran and Anglican), the piety of the religious picture rather than the liturgical symbol remained and took on new forms of life. Moreover, in the Roman Catholic Church, the 'Stations of the Cross' (which also came from Jerusalem) enabled individual worshippers to repaint the pictures of Jesus on his way to the cross; this could be done at any stage in the year, though it was usually a Lenten devotion. Another popular

6

development was the 'Three Hours' Devotion', which began in Peru in the seventeenth century, under Jesuit influence, and which gained popularity in many Anglican circles in the nineteenth. Once more, representational piety proves its ability to reach people. Perhaps the most eloquent expression of this kind of religious experience is to be found in Isaac Watts' hymn, 'When I survey the wondrous cross', which was originally written for the Eucharist, but which many Christians sing fervently in Holy Week as a genuinely profound meditation on Calvary, explicit, sentimental, grasping for redemption.

Christians living in the twentieth century inherit many of these religious approaches, as well as provide their own assimilation. Thus it comes as no surprise that all these pieties are alive among different sections of the Christian community. Popular piety persists in being representational in its character, which is why so many folk liturgies and family services in Holy Week reproduce the whole *dramatis personae* of the play in question, whether it is a donkey on Palm Sunday or a Jesus walking to trial and crucifixion. A more sophisticated piety exists among those who find these re-enactments tedious, perhaps even simplistic, and who want to be left alone to grow in their faith, through a liturgy that celebrates in code and symbol, instead of picture and drama. Finally, there are those who find the apologetic demands of Holy Week 'events' too great to bear, who feel their integrity prejudiced if they are to sit through endless representations, and who can only really take in a single celebration of death and resurrection, of Christian *Pasch*, of watch and renewal. Although the old Easter Vigil may not mean much to them, its theology, at least in its pristine form, offers precisely what they are looking for.

The bulk of modern liturgical texts, whether Roman Catholic, Anglican, or JLG, are rememorative in character, and seek to bring simple symbolism back into the corporate religious consciousness of an age that needs to learn anew what it is to worship imaginatively. It is interesting that whereas today most Roman Catholics worship on Good Friday at the new form of the traditional liturgy, with the reading of the passion and the veneration of the cross, the majority of their forebears attended a service of the Stations of the Cross, perhaps with hymns and a sermon. Here we have yet more evidence of the common ground that exists between many Christians today. For the Church of England, the new anthology of material for this holy season will find its own 'ambiance' in ordinary congregations insofar as the texts can be adapted to local circumstances. History can teach us that of the three pieties, the representational is the one that can get out of hand most easily, and the rememorative can become lifeless when the people find the symbolism burdensome. The new Church of England material is essentially rememorative in character. To that material we now turn.

2 The 1986 Directory

A Book for the whole Church

Lent, Holy Week, Easter is the result of the careful scholarly work of the Church of England's Liturgical Commission. The Commission members and their consultants represent a wide variety of styles of Christian worship within the Church of England. They have been sensitive to the needs of the whole Church, and not simply to one or another narrower group within it. It is not a 'party' book any more than the Commission which produced it is a 'party' commission. Part of the complexity at some points in the services it has provided has resulted from a desire to take seriously the particular sensitivities of different groups, and to produce a book that all may use with loyalty and real enthusiasm.

The Chairman of the Commission, in his Introduction, explains that the Commission had 'not sought to be innovative'. Certainly it is true that there is little in the way of original composition, though there is a good deal of improvement through redrafting of previously published material, and some material, such as the litany in the second Penitential Service and some of the Intercessory prayers, are new and will be widely welcomed. But if the Commission has not been innovative in the question of service order and structure, and in what it has included or excluded, that is only because there is nothing new in liturgy; somebody has always done it before, and if you dig deep enough you find your precedent. In the later chapters, it will emerge where the Commission dug and what it found. It would be easier to accuse the Commission of innovation than to suggest that it was slavish in its following of other modern revisions. In relation to the Roman Catholic Holy Week liturgy, much of which has been used, in the absence of authorized texts, by Anglicans who at other points of the year have not resorted much to the Roman Missal to supplement their normal

9

liturgical diet, the Commission has taken over a good deal of material, but has taken an independent line at certain key points of structure – the order of Intercession and Proclamation of the Cross on Good Friday, for instance, or of Vigil Readings and Service of Light in the Easter Liturgy. It has done this, not for the sake of being different, but because it believes it has found a more satisfying way within the tradition. It has had the advantage of working twenty years later than the Roman liturgical reformers and of being able to draw on the experience of those years. It was also aware that Roman Catholic liturgy is not as uniform as the average Anglican imagines, and experiment has been going on in that communion as in our own.

If *Lent, Holy Week, Easter* is not a party book, nor is it exclusively a book for great churches with fine liturgical and musical traditions. It *can* be used in such settings and, if it is, could renew some Holy Week ceremonies that have grown stale, unconvincing and not a little eccentric in some of our cathedrals and famous parish churches. They will, no doubt, welcome some authoritative guidance in an area where too much has been left to local enterprise. But *Lent, Holy Week, Easter* can be used as effectively in very ordinary parish churches, rural and urban, where nothing 'ambitious' has ever been attempted for Holy Week. The services do not assume a host of ministers, servers and massed choirs. Provision is made for choirs and music, but much that may be sung can also be said, and often popular hymns substituted for more difficult new material. Though there is scope for ceremonial with crucifer, acolytes and the like, even the Easter celebration, which is probably the most complicated of the services, can be undertaken in a church where the personnel will consist only of a priest, a handful of lay folk prepared to read, and a couple of people, not necessarily dressed up in distinctive gear, ready to hold and carry things. *Lent, Holy Week, Easter* is for all churches, whatever their size, resources, tradition or personnel. The chapters that follow here are intended to help churches of very different styles, and with very different expectations, to make the best of these services.

Nor need the use of these services be restricted to churches where Holy Communion Rite A is the norm. They have been drawn up with that context primarily in mind, but at the point where the service returns to the usual eucharistic shape, Holy Communion Rite B could equally well be used. There would of course be a move from modern liturgical English to the quasi-archaic liturgical language of Rite B, but, though we may wish services could have a uniformity of language, we have grown used to two styles side by side, not least in hymnody, and, in practice, it does not seem to detract over much from the sense of worship. A note in any case provides for the substitution of traditional musical texts where appropriate.

As its Introduction explains, *Lent, Holy Week, Easter* is a 'directory'. It is not a book to be used straight through, but an anthology to be dipped into, and adapted imaginatively to the local situation, but always with regard to the sane and scholarly good sense that can be gleaned from the introductions to each service as much as for the orders and texts themselves.

The 1986 Services: Some Common Features

There are a number of features in *Lent, Holy Week, Easter* which need to be noted, apart from the essentially re-memorative character which they share. First, like many modern liturgical texts, they assume a wide degree of *participation*. This does not apply just to the prayers and responses, but to the inner meaning of the services. Although provision is made for introductions to the special ceremonies, we are beginning to learn how good liturgy can become very bad worship when too many explanations are offered, usually ill-prepared (it takes a lot of preparation to seem to speak 'off the cuff'). There are other means of preparing folk for special liturgies, such as house-groups, parish magazines, and (for choir and servers) rehearsals.

Secondly, they set out to integrate the special ceremonies into the heart of the liturgy. Thus, the act of penitence (with or without the ashing), takes place at the end of the liturgy of the Word on Ash Wednesday, and the foot-washing occupies a similar position on Maundy Thursday. (In times past, the ashing would precede the Mass, and the foot-washing - if done at all -

11

would follow it.) It is important that presidents and preachers exploit such a position to the full. However, it has meant that the intercession runs the risk of becoming a passenger, because of its normal position at the end of the Word in the Sunday Eucharist. Perhaps there is good reason to lament the lack of provision for short intercessions in the eucharistic prayers of the ASB.

Thirdly, these new services allow considerable flexibility of shape. Thus, for example, we have already noted that the 'proclamation of the cross' on Good Friday precedes the intercessions, though it may follow them. Similarly, the ceremonies of light at Easter may come either *before* or *after* the eucharistic readings, though there is a preference for the latter. Such variation is in line with the provisions of the ASB, where in many of the services, *alternative structures* are permissible (e.g. offertory prayers at the Eucharist, and the signing with the cross at baptism). While variation of shape may be desirable for regular services (e.g. penitence at the Eucharist), it is doubtful whether it is wise to encourage it on special occasions; perhaps these new services would have more coherence if *shape* were *mandatory*. In this way, individual items can vary within a common framework without causing confusion, and rhythm be more easily identified by ordinary worshippers.

Fourthly, the lections for these services have been carefully worked out. Although the Sunday readings of ASB are an adaptation of the two-year JLG scheme, the influence of the Roman lectionary is obvious on the services of Holy Week, where the readings either follow a three-year scheme (as on Palm Sunday and Easter Day) or else they do not vary at all from year to year (Maundy Thursday and Good Friday). Ash Wednesday, on the other hand, which has invariable readings in the Roman rite, has variable ones in ASB, and these appear in the new services. There is considerable scope for the thoughtful preacher both in the matter of choice and in the preparation of sermons.

Fifthly, the services have many of the options in ASB 'Rite A' Eucharist for seasonal use. Thus, special sentences are provided. New forms for introducing the Peace are suggested. The blessing usually begins with a special, biblically-inspired formula. Moreover, Post-Communion prayers are provided for Ash Wednesday, Palm Sunday, Maundy Thursday, Good Friday, and Easter. The Ash Wednesday prayer is an adaptation of a prayer attributed to Anselm (taken from David Silk's *Prayers for Use at the Alternative Services*), whereas the two alternatives for Maundy Thursday adapt from the new Roman Missal (itself a derivative of the 'Gothic Missal'), and from the traditional Corpus Christi Collect attributed to Thomas Aquinas. Using sources in this way helps to build up a sense of liturgy as a creative use of history and an imaginative response to the present.

Finally, the language of many of the prayers is more fulsome and intimate than many other modern compositions. This holds true both of those (principal) services which we shall discuss in some detail as well as those devotional and domestic offices contained in the new anthology which we shall not be able to look at in quite the same way. Perhaps those people who find many modern prayers too clinical in style and cold in content may take comfort in these rather more rhetorical compositions, which have been specially brought together for use at this solemn stage in the liturgical year.

Lent and Easter in the Parish

Although it is commonplace to talk of Lent as a time for growing close to Christ, and though everybody knows that that nearly always involves time and space for reflection and growth, Lent can be the busiest, most overloaded period of the Christian year, and Holy Week an intimidating climax to it. It is partly that we tend to put on extra services on top of full parish programmes that we have already often supplemented for Lent with house groups or study courses of various kinds. We need to ask whether Lent is not, very often, more about clearing space in diaries than about adding to commitments. But it is also partly that we tend to overload the early part of Lent, or even the early part of Holy Week, with services, so that, by the time we reach Maundy Thursday, Good Friday and Easter, people are tiring. Lent needs to have sufficient incentive about it that it brings people to Holy Week with heightened emotions and expectations and with freshness. *Lent, Holy Week, Easter* believes that a special Ash Wednesday rite will help, as will a Penitential Service or two, and it relies on a sensitive use of the ASB Sunday provision, but it does not overdo its demands. There is wisdom in that. There is wisdom also in not giving a high profile to the Monday, Tuesday and Wednesday of Holy Week. They do not need a distinctive and special service, though the Church's round of worship in Eucharist and office will strengthen those who come to share in them, and undue emphasis on them, as if they were of equal significance with Palm Sunday, Maundy Thursday and Good Friday, will not help in ensuring that these great days are celebrated adequately by the whole church community. Planning Lent and Holy Week to reach the climax at the proper time, with just the right amount of preparation and build up requires planning and sensitivity; 'over kill' is a real danger.

Keeping up, and indeed building up, momentum is an important feature of both the seasons that come within the compass of this book - Lent and Easter. Lent is not a static season; it moves towards Holy Week, and every day that climax should feel closer and the people more prepared for it. The Sunday lectionary in The Alternative Service Book, with its distinct but related themes, aids this sense of development, and it will very often be best to resist that Anglican habit of thinking up series of Lent sermons or discussions that divide conveniently into six parts, but which have very little to do with preparation for Holy Week and Easter. This is not a time of the year to abandon the liturgical cycle with its sensitivity to mood and season. If that is true of Lent, it is all the more so of Eastertide, that great Fifty Days of celebration that lasts, uninterrupted, until Evening Prayer on Pentecost Sunday. It is rare to find an Anglican church taking Easter as seriously as Lent. Though the one may be seen as a forty day fast, the other is at best a couple of weeks of exuberance and then quickly 'back to normal'. A rediscovery of the integrity and development of the Easter *season* could be as great a benefit from *Lent, Holy Week, Easter* as the adoption of any particular service, though

14

the path was paved in The Alternative Service Book with its careful choice of Easter lections and its special Easter provision in the Eucharist. In general, the rediscovery of the liturgical shape of the Christian year, with its moods and cycles, that respond to feelings and experiences deep within us, accompanied by a wariness about special observances, Sundays dedicated to particular causes and other intrusions, would greatly deepen the Church's experience of worship all through the year, but especially from Ash Wednesday to Pentecost.

The planning of this period in parish life is not just an exercise with the diary and a concern to make the right choices to keep up the liturgical momentum, important as these are. Another part of the exercise is to be in the church building itself working out how the liturgy can fit into it. This is not just a matter of rehearsal a day or two before a particular service, though that is quite essential if these once-a-year services are to be a genuine help to devotion, and part of the diary exercise is to ensure that servers, organist, readers, sidesmen and other personnel can get together to prepare for worthy acts of worship. But, more than that, taking the church building seriously means considering which of the options in *Lent, Holy Week, Easter* make more sense in a particular building and what opportunities the building provides to enhance the liturgy. At this stage of the year, a church building that often seems a liability - a great barn of a church, for instance, with a small congregation almost lost within it - may suddenly come into its own, for the services of Holy Week cry out for movement and can be enriched by space to do and see. But it will mean getting the congregation out of their pews and to see movement and procession as something they *do*, rather than *watch*, in the liturgy. In Holy Week the building is hardly ever a liability. A small over-full little church recaptures the intimacy of those days and, when it is *too* small, the liturgy can spill outside to carry branches on Palm Sunday and light the new fire at Easter. But a great Gothic church with wide aisles and long chancel can suddenly be *used* in a way that is not always possible, with the chancel the setting for footwashing on Maundy Thursday, the long nave coming into its own for the proclamation of the cross on Good Friday, and

15

the baptistry providing the setting for the renewal of vows in the Easter liturgy, and the congregation *on the move* through the week and discovering that that in itself can deepen their sharing of the experience of a Lord who rode into the city and walked to his crucifixion and, in between went or was taken from place to place - upper room, garden, high priest's house, Pilate's court, tomb.

Music for the New Services

Music plays an important part in the liturgy of Holy Week and Easter. This has always been true, and not only in places with a liturgical tradition. Indeed, it has often been in places where the liturgy is least helpful and imaginative at this season that the music has been the most moving and powerful, with oratorios and fine hymns filling the gap left by lack of liturgical provision. Some will think that one of the weakest points of the new book is that it does not include the music for its key anthems, such as those at the proclamation of the cross on Good Friday, or the *Exultet* at Easter. There are, of course, traditional musical settings for some of these, and, where the translations of the words differ, it is made clear that other versions may be sung. It is also true that these new services provide opportunity for new composition, and this is already beginning. The greatest need will be for simple sung forms for congregations with no choir, or one of limited ability. But, where the music for certain anthems seems beyond the resources of a particular congregation, there is no need to dismiss these services outright. Some of the texts are suitable, as they stand, to be *said*, as much as sung, and are set out responsorially, for leader and people. This applies, for instance, to the selection of anthems at the foot of the cross on Good Friday. Other texts need a little local adaptation before they can be used in this way, with a careful division between leader and people; the *Exultet* in the Easter liturgy is of this sort. Sometimes the right course will be to *substitute* a familiar hymn or anthem at some of these points. It is not difficult, for instance, to think of hymns to sing kneeling before the cross on Good Friday. But, more often, the right

16

course will not be substitution, but *addition*. For it would be a pity to lose the texts of such songs as The Reproaches or the *Exultet*, for they are absolutely right for the occasion for which they were written, and what they lose in only being *said* can be put right by rounding them off with a familiar congregational hymn or song that lifts the spoken words into a doxology. Particular suggestions are included in the chapters that follow.

A word needs to be said about psalmody. Not only does *Lent, Holy Week, Easter* make rich provision for use of psalms in all its services, but it urges that they be not omitted on these days. It is difficult to enter fully into the scriptural origins of what the Church is celebrating without including Psalm 69 on Palm Sunday, Psalm 22 on Good Friday and Psalm 118 at Easter, and these are only three of many psalms that call out for inclusion. In many churches, however, the use of psalms has almost disappeared. Where the Eucharist is the only popular form of service, and where the invitation to include psalmody within it on a regular basis has not been taken up, the provision here, and the strong exhortation not to omit it, will be off-putting for some. But this need not be the case. First, there is the option of *saying* the psalms, quietly and reflectively and, probably, seated. This will be quite in tune with the spirit of Holy Week. But, second, there is the variety of ways in which the psalms may be sung. Anglican chant or the older plain chant are not the only possibilities, for all the beauty of both well done (and the latter can be well done without great musical resources). In particular *Lent, Holy Week, Easter* has made provision for the psalms to be sung (or said) responsorially with the verses sung by a single cantor, or a small choir, and the congregation responding with a simple refrain. These are in the style of Laurence Bévenot, Joseph Gelineau, Gregory Murray and others, and are meeting a real need in the Church. They are one of the ways in which the rich treasury of the psalter is being reintroduced to a new generation of worshippers. One good singer is all that is needed; the smallest congregation can usually produce that. In a different style is *Psalm Praise*, another way of making the psalms available to congregations that do not respond to traditional styles. For many churches, Ash Wednesday, Holy

17

Week and Easter may provide the impetus to take a fresh look at the psalms and to find in each community the most satisfactory way of incorporating them into worship.

Reading the Scriptures

Tables of readings do not attract and the reader may be tempted to pass over the pages of these in *Lent, Holy Week, Easter*. In so doing the reader would miss important information and opportunity. A new lectionary for Holy Week and Easter Week is given here, departing from that in the ASB quite considerably. The notes at the beginning of the Lectionary pages are very clear and repay careful examination.

But the principal change is in providing three alternatives at all the key points during Holy Week. Numbered A, B and C, they indicate a principal synoptic gospel to be followed through the period, with supporting matter from the other two. A church may opt to use the same one every year (and so end up with a balance not significantly different from the ASB's use of Mark) or to use the three in rotation through a three-year cycle. The latter will have a wide appeal. The provisions also include, as an alternative, shorter gospels for the Monday, Tuesday and Wednesday in Holy Week, where a gospel story describing an incident related to the day is preferred to another full passion reading.

Entering into a Drama

We have already seen that the great services of Holy Week are, to some extent, the early amalgamation of two traditions: one a single paschal celebration through Easter night and morning, the other a series of services remembering and celebrating the successive events of the week. Be that as it may, the amalgamation has long been complete and has acquired a shape and a coherence of its own. What we have is a great four part drama - Palm Sunday, Maundy Thursday, Good Friday, Easter - and, although each act in the drama can stand alone, and each, in some way or other, does celebrate the whole passion and

18

glimpse the resurrection, a real entering into our Lord's experience, and identifying with him at every point, requires attendance at all four parts of the total drama. Something is lost for anyone who misses one act; much is lost if a church congregation omits one service altogether. If it makes sense not to 'overload' people through Lent, and in the early days of Holy Week, it is in order that they may be urged to share in the liturgy of the four key days as a matter of the first priority. Let the liturgy of that week unfold, to faithful people returning for each successive part of the drama of their salvation, and they will find themselves moved at depths they have not often known, and experience an identification of their own story with that of our Lord in his passion that will transform both worship and Christian living throughout the year. The priest and the parish fail when they do not make this experience available in as compelling a way as possible to all the people they serve.

But, before Holy Week with its four part drama, comes Ash Wednesday, the beginning of Lent. It is to this first of the services in *Lent, Holy Week, Easter* that we must now turn.

3 Lent

Origins and Background

According to the ASB, Lent begins on Ash Wednesday, but it is
not clear when it ends. This is a problem shared with the
American Episcopal Book of Common Prayer (1979). The
Roman Missal (1970), by contrast, indicates clearly when the
season reaches its conclusion, because the period which starts
with Maundy Thursday evening Eucharist and ends on Easter
Day is called 'The Easter Triduum'. A simple calculation which
starts with Ash Wednesday and ends on Maundy Thursday
produces the startling conclusion that Lent lasts forty-*four*
days, instead of the traditional forty. Why the discrepancy?

The answer lies in the fact that Lent was not originally about
fasting for forty days exactly, in order to relive the experience
with Christ. As we have already seen, this is a later piety. The
origin of Lent lies, rather, in the simple expedient of having a
time of preparation (which included fasting) before the great
festival. The length of this preparation varied (and still does)
among the various churches. The special associations of Lent in
antiquity, however, have left a permanent mark on the season
which no recent revisions have been able to eradicate, even if
they wanted to. To fast before a feast is the most natural thing
in the world. Any great event gains in psychological impact if
there is a time of withdrawal and reflection beforehand on the
part of those who want to enter into its true meaning.

The special associations of Lent are: the period of fasting on
the part of the faithful, the final preparation of those who were
to be baptized at Easter, and the time of penitence observed by
those who were excluded from communion for some grievous
sin, and who were to be reconciled before Easter. All three
features intermingled; baptismal candidates fasted, and the
Lenten liturgy exerted a penitential mood on everyone who
worshipped. But the three features are distinct, and no one can

understand the meaning of Lent without probing into their proper purpose.

Among the many preachers of antiquity, the one who stands out as a remarkable witness to Lent as a means of spiritual growth for *all* Christians is Leo the Great. Apart from fasting, but no doubt as a result of it, the ordinary Christian can 'scrutinize himself, and search severely his inmost heart; let him see that no discord cling there, no wrong desire be harboured'. Lent, however, does not end in soul-searching, however agonizing Leo's recommendations might become. The faithful should look to their neighbours: 'Let us rejoice in the replenishment of the poor, whom our bounty has satisfied. Let us delight in the clothing of those whose nakedness we have covered with needful raiment.' Apart from such works of mercy, Leo asks his hearers to abstain from wantonness, drunkenness, the lusts of the flesh, and much else besides. For he is convinced that 'it is by such observances . . . that God's mercy will be gained, the charge of sin wiped out, and the adorable Easter festival doubly kept'.

Sharp words, indeed, from a fifth-century preacher. It is interesting that during his lifetime, the Roman liturgy of baptism was becoming increasingly adapted to the current trend, which moved away from adult candidates to infants. This brings us to the second traditional feature of Lent. Much has been made in recent years of the baptismal character of Easter. Many of the old Lenten and Eastertide readings and collects (in the 1662 Book of Common Prayer as well as the 1570 Missal) contain signs of the importance attached to baptism in antiquity and the involvement of the whole Christian community in its celebration. It is, indeed, a sign of the poverty of our baptismal spirituality that, when Roman Catholics were allowed once more (after many centuries of haphazard anticipation or neglect) to celebrate the Easter Vigil on Saturday night, they had to be given a new custom, the renewal of baptismal promises, in order to build up a corporate understanding of baptism as a sacrament of solidarity with other Christians and a lifelong growth into Christ. In antiquity, such an innovation would have been unnecessary. Moreover, it was not just the actual baptism celebration which was viewed in this way, it was the entire Lenten liturgy. In the fourth and fifth centuries, those who were to be baptized at Easter were enrolled at the start of Lent, and underwent an intense course of Christian nurture, as the culmination of their previous preparation. This involved learning parts of the Gospels, the Creed, and the Lord's Prayer (the last two had to be rendered publicly towards the end of Lent). Preaching the baptismal homilies was a great honour in some religious centres, like Antioch, where both John Chrysostom and Theodore of Mopsuestia had this privilege while both were presbyters. Those to be baptized were 'catechized' in this way, and were often called 'catechumens' (= 'those being catechized'). Good preachers took care to differentiate what they said about liturgies of baptism and Eucharist *before* the great event and what they said *afterwards*, since (in those days) only the baptized could attend the whole Eucharist.

Perhaps because much that is wholesome, dynamic, and rich in this period of antiquity has inspired theologians and liturgists in our century, we are learning (in our own different circumstances) to appropriate some of this approach to baptism. The new Roman Rite for the Initiation of Christian Adults *assumes* that the public liturgies of Lent and Easter will involve ordinary Sunday congregations, and that the 'normal' liturgy for Christian Initiation will be the baptism and confirmation at the Easter Vigil. Such a restoration is far-off, although there are some Anglican parishes which do their best to attempt it, even to the extent that they import a tame bishop for the Easter Vigil. Nonetheless, much Western Christianity does need a corporate counterbalance to the centuries of individualism which we have all inherited. One of the ways of doing this is to make Lent and Easter a time for spiritual renewal, based on the baptismal liturgy, so that any 'renewal of baptismal vows' which is carried out at the festival itself is not yet more 'words, mere words', but is the climax to some hard thinking and soul-searching. Leo the Great, being dead, yet speaketh!

The third feature of Lent is the one which is perhaps nearest to the expectations of ordinary Christians, though perhaps not in the way the new services have been put together. Penitence is a difficult theme to express in modern liturgies, because we live in an age which (religiously) is reacting against what is lampooned as Victorian piety ('doom and gloom'), but which (internationally) is living under the threat of nuclear war and possible extinction. Modern liturgies which stress 'celebration' mix strangely with the atmosphere of international peace negotiations! And yet this is precisely the point of tension at which Christians are called to live. To use words like 'celebration' does not exclude penitence. The liturgy for the 'Beginning of Lent', as well as the penitential services for the season of Lent, are framed with precisely this in view. They are intended to make a special focus on penitence and renewal.

There was in antiquity a custom which grew up, probably in the third century, of isolating certain grave sins as being of such significance that the person concerned needed to unburden himself, to be excluded from communion for a time, and to be reconciled with the Church at a later date. Rigorous as this scheme is, it nonetheless expresses the *social* character of sin, and the *corporate* nature of the Church. Once again, the dynamic model of the Church redresses the individualistic image that we in the West have imbibed. In time, such an 'order of penitents' was established. They left the church building at the end of the liturgy of the word, together with the catechumens; but, unlike them, they had already been baptized, and therefore sought to renew their spiritual lives by continued fasting and prayer.

The Gelasian Sacramentary, which probably (here) reflects liturgical usage at Rome in the sixth century, has a series of five prayers which are said over the penitents on the Wednesday between what is called Quinquagesima and Quadragesima. On the Thursday before Easter, at a special mass for the reconciliation of penitents, there is a special set of prayers after the gospel for those being reconciled to the Church. There could be no clearer demonstration than this that Lent was a season of penitence for this special group. It was no doubt from the popular practice of rubbing ash on the body (and wearing a hairshirt) that the later custom arose of ashing these penitents at the start of Lent. By the ninth century, such public penitence was exceptional, as private forms of penitence became more popular, and from this time, ashing started to be observed as a custom for *any* Christian, with the result that ashing became separated from the liturgy of public penitence. Such a development seems logical in itself. If people are 'going to confession' (i.e. confessing sins *privately*) and doing so at *any* time of the year, then there is no need for public exclusion from the Church at the beginning of Lent, to be followed by a set time of penitence, and final reconciliation with the Church on Maundy Thursday. On the other hand, there would be much to be said for making Lent a penitential season and using a well-worn outward sign for such a mood.

So Ash Wednesday liturgies develop in various ways, resulting in elaborate rites before the main Mass. Sometimes the old name 'in capite jejunii' (= 'at the beginning of the fast') persists. Sometimes the new name 'die cinerum' (= 'on the day of ashes') is adopted. On the other hand, at Narbonne in the twelfth century, there are *two* ashings, the first being part of the main rite leading up to the solemn extrusion of the penitents from the church doors, the second being a general ashing, of the rest of the congregation. The earliest form for blessing the ashes dates from the tenth century, in the Romano-Germanic Pontifical, written in Mainz, *c.*AD 950. This includes the formula at the giving of the ash, 'Remember that you are dust' (Gen. 3.19), which is used invariably in the Roman books, down to the present day.

The pattern represented by Narbonne is, clearly, a relic, though there are vestiges of the 'double ashing', together with the persistence of the older public rite of penitence in later books. Indeed, the Roman Pontifical (1596) contains both an order for ashing and excluding penitents at the beginning of Lent and their reconciliation on Maundy Thursday. Pontificals, however, being bishops' books, are generally conservative in character. Moreover, we may also observe that the earlier rigorous customs required the bishop's presence, whereas private penitence and general ashing did not. Such are the ways liturgy expresses changing circumstances and relationships.

These medieval rites of ashing (with or without extrusion) were no mere preludes to the Eucharist. They involved such liturgical features as the singing of the litany, the seven penitential psalms, and the preaching of a sermon on the theme of the day. One feature of note is that they frequently have an 'absolutio', which is similar to the shorter form at Mattins and Evensong in the Scottish Prayer Book (1929). This prayer grants forgiveness, as well as 'time for true repentance' and 'amendment of life'. Prayers of reconciliation on Maundy Thursday stress the completion of this repentance and amendment of life, as well as the ecclesial character of this special reconciliation.

At the Reformation, a new service was compiled for the Prayer Book, called 'A Commination' Although the term 'commination' appears to have been used for the first time in the second half of the fifteenth century (and was therefore, for Cranmer, a recent term), the rite itself is an interesting adaptation of the medieval Ash Wednesday rite. It begins with a short introduction, which leads into a series of denunciations of certain sins; a homily is read; Psalm 51 (one of the seven penitential psalms) follows; and the service concludes with the Lord's Prayer and suffrages, and some prayers compiled from medieval and biblical sources. The service was obviously intended to adapt its Latin predecessor to new needs, and it is noteworthy that the ashing and the Eucharist have disappeared, perhaps because the ashing was thought superstitious and not many folk communicated on this day.

Modern Ash Wednesday Liturgies

In recent years, the ashing has been reintroduced. Tractarian Missals adapt (or simply include) material from the Roman Missal (1570). On the other hand, the *Directory of Ceremonial* (1930) suggests that it be included after the prayer, 'O most mighty God', near the end of the Commination service. The *Directory* notes this prayer's Latin sources, and also recommends that the Eucharist follow it immediately. Such a restoration is entirely in accord with the *Directory*'s intention of adapting Prayer Book services to judicious Catholic practices.

However, the new Roman Missal (1970) changes things entirely. Instead of the ashing taking place *before* Mass, it finds its place within the liturgy of the Word, after a homily. The ashes are blessed, first of all, and two prayers are provided which rewrite their medieval originals to give them a more positive and less depressed view of the Lenten penance. The ashes are imposed, *either* with a new formula ('Repent and believe in the Gospel' – Mark 1.15) or the traditional one ('Remember you are dust' – Gen. 3.19). The Eucharist continues with the prayer of the faithful.

The American Book of Common Prayer (1979) ingeniously adapts the new Roman order to what could be described as an Anglican ethos. After the sermon at the Eucharist, the president reads a short homily which explains the purpose of Lent. This is an adaptation of a recent Canadian form, and the new service for the Beginning of Lent takes its main inspiration from it. Then the American rite has an optional prayer over the ashes (i.e. the service can be celebrated *without* the imposition of ashes). Ashes may then be given, with the old Gen. 3.19 formula. Three penitential elements follow. The first is Psalm 51. The second is a 'Litany of Penitence', a new composition which is an explicit and positive form of general confession. The third is an adaptation of the absolution from the old Prayer Book Mattins and Evensong. The liturgy continues with the Peace.

The new rite adapts this American adaptation even further. After the introductory greeting, the president explains the meaning of Lent either in his own words or in a form adapted from the American book. (This is a new position, since the American version comes after the sermon.) After the readings and sermon, the service continues with part (or all) of the ASB litany. (The Litany may also come at the beginning.) Silence follows, and after a versicle and response, the long alternative ASB confession is said. (The confession is 'worked up to' on this day, as a central part of the liturgy.) At this point, the rite of ashing may be included. It begins with a simple explanation, which leads into an adaptation (and improvement?) of the American prayer over the ashes. (Neither version explicitly 'blesses' the ashes.) The ashes are given, either in silence, or in a formula which combines the two new Roman texts, the first one coming second, and having been adapted. Then, whether or not there has been ashing, the rite ends with two alternative prayers, one a collect for forgiveness, the other an absolution. The Eucharist continues with the intercessions and the peace. The new service builds on the strengths of the American version. It is important that 'ashing' does not seem to be mandatory, since for many Anglicans it is an unfamiliar rite. While the American version brings together penitence and ashing in a way compatible with Anglican tradition, it does not associate ashing so closely with absolution.

The new service is termed 'An Order for the Beginning of Lent', and it is directed for use either on Ash Wednesday or on the First Sunday in Lent. For reasons of conservatism as against consistency, modern revisions have kept Ash Wednesday as the start of Lent. Thus the new permission for this liturgy to be celebrated on the First Sunday, though it may have been intended to meet pastoral necessity, in the rural church for instance, does give some support to the view that, if we *are* to have forty days, the season anciently called Quadragesima should really start on that Sunday. As we have already indicated, Lent has had many variations in its duration. Early Roman tradition knew simply a three-week fast. By the latter half of the fourth century, however, the period was extended to last six weeks, and thus make up forty days. Preparation for Easter thus had two stages, the season of Lent which could be said to end on Maundy Thursday, and the Easter 'Triduum' ('three days') beginning on Maundy Thursday evening and ending on Easter Day itself. The fast of forty days, however, is *not* coextensive with Lent, since Lent includes Sundays, which cannot properly be called fast days. Similarly, the importance attached to the 'Triduum' is an indication of the desire to hold together the actions leading up to the Last Supper, arrest, trial, crucifixion, death, burial, and resurrection of Christ.

In the face of such complexity, it may reasonably be asked, why the extra days, and Ash Wednesday? The answer lies in the love of asceticism, and the desire among many folk to extend Lent even further than its first Sunday. The immediate result was to make the preceding Wednesday and Friday into rigorous fast days. (This love of rigour was also responsible for the 'mini-Lent' which subsequently became Septuagesima, Sexagesima, and Quinquagesima Sundays, which were abolished after the Second Vatican Council.) However, once the extra rigour was accepted, and because Sundays and major feasts could not be counted as fast-days, the tradition grew up, from the seventh century, that Lent began on the Wednesday after Quinquagesima, and embodied forty fast-days (interrupted by six Sundays) which ended on Holy Saturday. The key to the riddle lies in the fact that forty days of *fasting* requires such a scheme, whereas forty days as forty days (no more) can be calculated from the First Sunday until Maundy Thursday.

One question which rears its head among congregations which adopt the ceremony of ashing: where do we get the ashes from? The answer most frequently given is that the remaining palm crosses from the previous year are burnt, and worked into a paste which leaves an adequate mark on the forehead of the penitent believer. Such a practice has an obvious symbolism. Christians acclaim their Saviour as Lord and King but only a few days later nail him to the cross. Consequently, our ambivalence is a symptom of our need of forgiveness. In fact, burning the palms is a relatively recent custom. In the fourteenth-century Lyon rite, it is clearly stated that the ashes 'are made in some churches from the blessed branches of the previous year, if they are available'. Providing the ashes in this way was clearly optional, and (it should be noted) the 'blessed branches' would have been from local trees, rather than Mediterranean palms, even in Lyon. Sometimes liturgy seems more fanciful than it is originally intended to be.

Using the 1986 Service

'The Order for the Beginning of Lent' in *Lent, Holy Week,*

Easter shows signs of overloading. Material has been banished to an appendix and other material made optional so that this may be avoided, but one can still detect a desire on somebody's part to put too much in. It is easy to understand why. Ash Wednesday provides the principal day in the year on which the rich treasury of penitential material in the Anglican tradition, much of it neglected in the ordinary run of things in today's church, may be given an 'airing'. The Ten Commandments, the Litany, the greatest of penitential psalms, 51, all seem to demand a place and all could certainly contribute to the ethos of the day. But just as the service writers resisted the temptation to build the maximum material into the mainstream text, so, in the parish, those who plan the use of this service need to have the same discipline if the rite is not to become long and wordy. When there are too many words, the first thing to go is silence, and the notes for this service lay particular emphasis on the inclusion of a good deal of silence for reflection as 'an integral part of the rite'.

The setting for this service that the Commission clearly had in mind is the Eucharist celebrated as it would normally be on Sunday, but here celebrated on Ash Wednesday, probably, in most communities, in the evening. Provision is made for the use of the material without Holy Communion, and this will be necessary in some, especially rural, settings when the priest cannot be in five places at once on Ash Wednesday, though the provision for the use of this service on the First Sunday in Lent is also designed to meet his problem. The Ash Wednesday rite, without Holy Communion, need not be a second best unsatisfactory service. Ash Wednesday begins a fast and that can be symbolized by the abstinence from Communion, and the very incompleteness of the service without the eucharistic ending can be the pointer to the fact that something has been begun, rather than accomplished. Nevertheless, where possible, the sharing in the Eucharist is the natural climax, with ceremony on this occasion restrained and music perhaps minimal, in contrast to the previous Sunday.

For contrast with the rest of the Christian year, and especially with the joyful Eastertide that will follow it, is an important mark of the Lenten season. This opening service may be used to make that contrast dramatically right at the beginning. The Introduction to this service makes mention of what should be 'given up' - *gloria*, *alleluia*, some use of organ, flowers, though it is important to keep in mind that contrast and austerity are what is required, and never gloom and despondency. But with the disappearance of the 'Gesima' Sundays as a sort of semi-Lent, Ash Wednesday, with its sudden change of mood and colour, is able to make its impact quite dramatically, if this service is ordered sensitively.

The service may open, of course, with a hymn (section 1). It is nearly always right to do so, for a hymn has the power to draw individuals into relationship and worship as effectively as any words the president may say. But on this day there is an argument for an entry in silence and the sentence and greeting without hymn, canticle or psalm first. In this way the first congregational singing would, appropriately, be the words of Psalm 51 (section 8) after the first reading. When a hymn is used, here or later in the service, the neglected and stark 'office hymns' that the more traditional hymn books include (see, for instance, AMR 85, 'Jesu, who this our Lententide') can sometimes capture the austere spirit of the day more than some of the more popular Lenten hymns.

After the Greeting (section 2), the president explains the meaning of Lent (section 3). This is simply a slightly longer and more formalized explanation of the theme of the service than many clergy today wisely insert at this point in the service. The particular text is fairly didactic and necessarily so since the real meaning and challenge of Lent is lost to many churchpeople for whom it has been reduced to a historical commemoration of our Lord's forty days in the wilderness. But where the material in this introduction will find a place in the sermon, or where this particular teaching has been well assimilated, a shorter and less formal form will be appropriate. In whatever precise form, this bidding leads very naturally into silent prayer and the collect (section 5). Few will probably take advantage of the rubric (section 4) to interpolate *Kyrie Eleison*, *Trisagion* or the Litany, though those who desire a long service, with both Litany and

Decalogue, will want to use the former at this point.

The Ministry of the Word makes the Old Testament Reading (section 7) mandatory in this service. All three passages provided, from which one is to be chosen, are sharp exhortations from the prophets and provide cutting edge to the day's liturgy, which is why this reading has been made mandatory. So has the psalm that follows, Psalm 51 (section 8), though whether it should be said or sung, and in what style, is a matter for local decision. Where said, it is better said quietly, reflectively, slowly and seated. New Testament Reading (section 9) and Canticle, Hymn or further Psalm (section 10) may follow, but all are optional. The Gospel (section 11) is then read and the sermon (section 12) follows it in the normal way. Because the sermon immediately precedes the special material in the service, 'The Liturgy of Penitence', it must clearly relate to, and lead into, this section, if there is not to be a break in the flow of the service.

The Liturgy of Penitence is a carefully devised form, moving through six stages, not all of them mandatory. They are (a) Bidding, (b) Litany (or Decalogue), (c) Silence, (d) Prayer of Confession, (e) Imposition of Ashes and (f) Concluding Prayer for Forgiveness. The rubrics instruct the people to kneel. ASB practice has been to restrict instruction about posture to those rare occasions where one such is overwhelmingly appropriate. This is one of those occasions. Humility and penitence are naturally expressed kneeling and, even where kneeling is not a normal part of the liturgy, it would be right to invite people to kneel here, if necessary talking about it first in the sermon.

The president invites the people to call to mind their sins and the infinite mercy of God (section 13). It is an invitation to which they might immediately respond in silent reflection, omitting section 14. But, unless the sermon has engendered just the right atmosphere for creative reflection, some words will be needed. The text provides the appropriate section of the ASB litany, which may be said or sung, and may appropriately be led by a minister kneeling 'in the midst of the people'. Others may prefer to use the Ten Commandments which are printed in the appendix, both in their straightforward form, with silence as the only response to each, and also in the form that includes a New Testament 'comment' on each, which is already found in the appendix of Holy Communion Rite A, though in the present text 'brothers' and 'men' have gone in the cause of eliminating 'exclusive' language.

Whether by the use of Litany or Commandments, in one form or another, or by the omission of all these in order to come more directly to section 15, the people are now brought to the silence with its concluding response. A note underlines that this is to be more than a mere pause. In a sense it is the heart of the day's distinctive liturgy. In some congregations it will be a natural thing, needing no explanation or introduction beyond the simple rubric, but in many churches, where the use of silence is at an early stage, the invitation will seem threatening and the time be wasted unless, in his sermon, the priest has given some indication of how such time can be used and indeed how long he intends it should be. If he is wise, he will use this occasion to teach how, in a smaller way, the penitential section in *every* Eucharist, can and should be an opportunity for silent personal recollection of individual sin and failure drawn together in the spoken corporate confession that follows the silence. (But in all too many places, it isn't like that; bidding leads into confession without a pause for breath, let alone for thought.)

The words of confession (section 16) are from the appendix of Rite A, though the second line has been amended. A note allows the substitution of the usual text in use in the parish, but this is best resisted since different and special words are part of what makes this penitential section stand out as it should on Ash Wednesday. Apart from its difference, there is virtue also on this day that it is a little longer and richer in its imagery.

The Imposition of Ashes may now follow. It is much to be hoped that this simple ceremony will indeed be included in the service by many churches. Unlike much 'ritual' it does not require the conditions of a great church or a large 'altar party' or elaborate music. Indeed any of these could detract from its effectiveness. Where people are a little reluctant, they need to be told gently that a religion that responds enthusiastically to candles at Christmas and palms in Holy Week, because of their celebratory character, but is suspicious of ash for Lent, with its penitential character, sounds an imbalanced and perhaps unrealistic religion. After a brief invitation, the President says a prayer over the ashes (section 17). A note elsewhere mentions the practice of burning the palms or other branches from the previous year, but that is not in any way an essential part of the procedure.

The rubrics do not specify whether the people come to the minister, or he to them, for the Imposition of the Ashes, nor do they specify posture. Local circumstances will dictate what is best. In most traditional settings, it will be appropriate for the congregation to come forward to the altar rail, but perhaps to adopt a different posture from that at the Communion. In other small and less formal settings, where people sit in a circle or semi-circle, the minister may come to them. With his or her thumb, the minister makes the sign of the cross in ash on the forehead of each, having first received the same sign from another, in order that this ministry may clearly be seen to be the ministry of one sinner to another. This may all be done with no words at all, but the rubric at section 18 (together with an earlier note) expresses a preference for the formula, 'Remember that you are dust, and to dust you shall return. Turn away from sin and be faithful to Christ.' In the Roman Rite these two sentences are alternatives, but here they are held together, the one rightly negative, the other positive, and both should be used. A note makes it clear that, as with the distribution of Holy Communion, more than one minister, ordained or lay, may be used for this ministry if numbers require it. Meanwhile, a hymn or an anthem is permitted, but, again, silence will often seem the better option.

The Liturgy of Penitence concludes with a Prayer for Forgiveness, though a note allows its omission altogether where there has been ash used, for that ceremony itself provides a natural climax for this distinctive part of the service, and more words may seem superfluous. Where a prayer is used, two alternatives are given. The first (section 20) is more a prayer for strength than an assurance of pardon. Its use would emphasize the character of Lent in which the spirit of penitence expressed in this service is carried forward through forty days of spiritual exercise. But a conventional absolution is also provided (section 21) for those who believe that should be the invariable response to confession. Interestingly it is printed in the 'us' rather than 'you' form (contrary to ASB practice), though with the alternative permitted, as the italics indicate. In the form printed, the minister would say these prayers kneeling with the people.

The main text would now rejoin the usual eucharistic order with the Peace, but a rubric permits additional material in the appendix. This is of two sorts. Those who are unhappy with a celebration without intercession may use the Rite A Litany of Intercession. But it should be said that, unless the other litany form has been omitted at both the earlier points, the service is in danger of being overloaded with this sort of material. Those with a particular affection for the Prayer of Humble Access may insert it here or use its alternative form from the Rite A appendix. All these texts are provided, and all are appropriate, but the move from the Liturgy of Penitence to the Peace is a smooth and logical one that has much to commend it. Thereafter the service follows the usual order. A special Post-Communion prayer (section 40) underlines the spirit of disciplined searching that will mark the Lenten season. The other seasonal and variable material is all from The Alternative Service Book.

As has already been noted, the service may be used on the First Sunday in Lent. When this does happen, some thought needs to be given to the choice of readings and, to some extent, all the 'propers' of the Sunday. On the one hand the introduction into this service of the Lent 1 wilderness/ temptation theme not only detracts from the unity of the rite, but actually emphasizes an association of ideas that liturgical reform of Lent has tried to play down. On the other hand, the Lent 1 readings are the first of a series taking us through the Sundays of Lent, and the integrity of that cycle needs to be preserved. Local decision making will be best in this instance.

In planning the use of this service on a Sunday, a parish will need to take seriously the fact that, for its effectiveness, this form relies heavily on an atmosphere of quiet, reflection and silence. That is not always achievable within some forms of family worship. How it may be done on this particular day needs to be carefully planned and not left to chance. It is equally important that what is established on Ash Wednesday is maintained and not dissipated through Lent. It is not a distinctive *day* that the Church needs, but a distinctive season, of stark simplicity and austerity, in worship as much as in anything else. Priest, organist and all concerned with the liturgy need to be conscious of the need to build on the Ash Wednesday experience, so that there is a steady movement towards the Passion as the weeks of Lent go by.

Services of Penitence

The new services include two forms of penitential offices, which may be used at any time in Lent (or at other times of the year). Both forms reflect the growing desire to make a special feature of penitence in this season, which is to be welcomed, since many complain that the new standard Eucharist sometimes lacks an adequate penitential note. (The Roman Catholic Church also has special penitential services in Lent.) Each form has an extended litany, the first one being based on the beatitudes, the second one dwelling on Christ's relationships with particular people, as recorded in the Gospels. These developments may well help to build up a new and healthy piety of penitence and renewal, and contribute greatly towards preparation for Easter.

A note indicates how these two services, which are identical in shape and emphasis, but not in content, may be combined with Holy Communion, but they are presented as services in their own rite without such a context. This is wise, since their primary use will be *in preparation for* a great festival and its Eucharist. There is no need for a priest for these services and there is no clear presidential role. There is not even any obvious reason for such a service to be in church - it would be entirely appropriate in, for instance, a house group. These services are not suitable for *regular* use, not even in Lent. One could not, for instance, build a weekly evening service around them. If the Ash

Wednesday rite has provided the penitential beginning to Lent, one of these might find an appropriate place in parish life in the fifth full week of Lent as a renewal of that penitence before entering into the experience of Holy Week. The use of one of these services on Monday, Tuesday or Wednesday in Holy Week itself can be envisaged in places where there is a heavy diet that week, but in most places that would be to overload the liturgical diary, and in the latter days of Holy Week the liturgy of each day has such a penitential flavour that these services would be superfluous. But, although they are printed within the Lent provision, they are not intended for use solely in that season and they could meet a need in many places on an evening soon before Pentecost or Christmas, with careful choice of lections, still penitential in character but to suit the season.

Whenever they are used, they are similar to the Ash Wednesday service in having silence as a principal component. In the same way that the Litany in the Ash Wednesday rite helps to create a spirit of penitence, which finds a natural continuation in a fairly long silence, before all is summed up in the corporate words of the confession, so in these services of penitence there is an identical sequence of litany, silence and corporate confession. These are quiet meditative services with great potential.

4   Palm Sunday

Eastern Origins

There are two aspects of Palm Sunday which belong together in the new liturgies. One is the fact that Jesus entered Jerusalem. The other is that he was crucified. In the Syrian rite, there is a charming old hymn which reflects this ambivalence, part of which contains the following strophes:

> Jacob tied an ass to a vine-stalk and waited.
> Then came Zechariah, who detached it and gave it to his Lord.
> The prophet gave it to his Lord, and he mounted it; and
> Zechariah walked before him, crying, 'Receive your king.'
>
> Zion said: 'Why does he come? I have not called him.'
> The prophet said: 'He is your king and he comes to reign.'
> Zion said: 'I do not want him to reign over me.'
> The prophet replied: 'He will reign over the Church,
>   and you, he will abandon.'
>
> Zion said: 'I will not open my doors to him, he will not enter.'
> The prophet replied: 'The Church will open her own,
>   and will receive him.'
> Zion said: 'If he enters my walls, I will crucify him.'
> The Prophet replied: 'But his cross is living,
>   and it will crush you.'

This little dialogue-meditation is part of a special hymn which is still sung before the blessing of the palms in the Syrian rite today. In a reflective and dramatic manner, the Church brings together Old and New Testaments, in order to affirm the fundamental spiritual paradox of Holy Week. Palm Sunday is, in one sense, an absurd affair. Zion's mind is closed, but the prophet's is not. The Church prefers her routine attitudes, but there is a voice in the wilderness ready to debunk tradition in order to point to a world turned upside down. 'But his cross is living, and it will crush you.'

Palm Sunday takes us to Jerusalem, for it is on Jerusalem soil that many of the special associations of Holy Week find their origin. But it is probable that the earliest practice (in both East and West) was to let the passion theme dominate the Eucharist on this Sunday before Easter. Perhaps for this reason the travel diary of Egeria takes careful note of Jerusalem practice on the afternoon of this day. 'At one o'clock [she writes] all people go up to the Eleona Church on the Mount of Olives', for a service which lasts until three, and from there they go to the Imbomon (the place from which Jesus is supposed to have ascended into heaven), for another service, which lasts until five. At its conclusion, the palm gospel is read from Matthew, and after this:

> the bishop and all the people rise from their places, and start off on foot down from the summit of the Mount of Olives. All the people go before him with psalms and antiphons, all the time repeating: 'Blessed is he that cometh in the name of the Lord'. The babies and the ones too young to walk are carried on their parents' shoulders. Everyone is carrying branches, either of palm or olive, and they accompany the bishop in the very way the people did when once they went down with the Lord. They go on foot all down the Mount to the city, and all through the city to the Anastasis [= the main church, of the resurrection], but they have to go pretty gently on account of the older women and men among them who might get tired.

Here is the earliest account of a palm liturgy. It is an outdoor exercise, which retraces the steps (supposedly) of Jesus and his followers. The branches carried are either palm or olive (an option reflected in several of the later medieval blessing prayers.) The atmosphere is a mixture of formal and informal. It is novel for the writer, and it cried out for adaptation in other parts of the Christian world.

This is precisely what happened, and in different ways. The Syrian rite (which we mentioned earlier) incorporates the palm gospel and procession right into the heart of the morning Eucharist. When such a synthesis was done is uncertain, but even though the passion narrative is not read, the tragic ambiance of the day is fully reflected in the little hymn, with its argumentative dialogue between Zion and Zechariah. After various lections (including Luke 19.29-40), the branches are blessed and distributed, and the procession moves out of church by a side door, and involves everyone. The procession re-enters church by the main door, and the Eucharist is taken up from its usual place, but after the reading of the Johannine palm narrative (John 12.12-22, a rare lection in the East and West). The Syrians clearly let the palm theme take over, but they keep the ambivalence of the day through another device, namely a penitential evening office, in a darkened (and undecorated) church, which involves another procession out through a side door, and in through the main entrance, this time with the door initially closed, as a sign of rejection. Movement and symbolism matter. The Byzantine rite, like the Syrians, has the palm gospel (John 12.1-18) as the main theme for the morning Eucharist, but whereas there was once a procession, it has long disappeared from use. Turning now to the West, we meet an already established practice at Rome of reading the canticle of Philippians (Phil. 2.5-11) and the Matthew passion narrative (Matt. 26—27) at the Eucharist on this day. Indeed, although it comes to be referred to as 'Palm' Sunday, there lingers a tradition in a few books which also calls it 'Passion' Sunday, which the new services attempt to introduce. The passion narratives, which are so central to the four Gospels, were all read in antiquity at various stages of Holy Week. In churches of the Roman rite, Matthew was read on the Sunday preceding Easter, John was read on Good Friday, and the other two were inserted on the intervening days, with Luke on Wednesday and Mark on Tuesday. The primacy of Matthew and John persisted through the Reformation, and is reflected in Lutheran tradition, which is known to many people through the music of Bach's two 'Passions'. In the later Middle Ages (after the adoption of the palm prelude to the Eucharist), the Matthew passion on this Sunday came to be read dramatically. This was a gradual process, the earliest stage of which was to have one reader (a deacon) who would vary the dynamics of his chant, in order to illustrate the narrative. By the tenth century, three deacons take over, one acting as narrator, another as Christ, the third as anyone else. The chant reached complex proportions as time went on. The same tradition (and elaboration) grew up on Good Friday with the Johannine passion narrative. All this serves to distinguish the passion narratives from any other gospel readings in the liturgical year. Modern revisions all reflect this dramatic penchant, although chant is replaced by congregational involvement, with the whole people of God 'acting' as the 'crowd'.

Palms in the West

But what of the palm theme? It is a moot point as to when it first appears in the Roman liturgy. Evidence suggests that it came to Rome *via* France, which would make much sense, since the liturgical 'trade-route' from the East often worked that way. On the other hand, since the old Roman books almost invariably call the day 'Sunday of palms', but the earliest prayers are all concerned with the passion, it is conceivable that people brought branches to church with them, but that these were not actually *blessed* until further influences arrived. In England, Aldhelm of Sherborne (705-9) refers to singing 'Hosanna' in Church on this day, and a century later, Amalarius of Metz testifies to a procession at Lyon. Earliest Roman evidence consists of a simple palm collect, but these occur in Sacramentaries used outside Rome itself, which is another indication of foreign influence. Indeed, the Gelasian Sacramentary of Gellone (later eighth century) contains a lengthy blessing of palms which recounts the story of Palm Sunday as well; the prayer is taken from the old Spanish rite.

Such foreign influence affords the kind of proof that the development of local liturgical customs in the Middle Ages was a complex business. The old Spanish rite of Toledo is a case in point, for here we are dealing with a native tradition, a native style of Latin, and an independence of any centralized authority in Rome. This rite prefixes the palm ceremonies to Eucharist, which had (unlike Rome, but like the East) a palm gospel; but it does so in a manner that suits an urban environment, starting in another church, and moving in procession to the main church for the Eucharist. In other respects, the old Spanish tradition reflects Jerusalem influence, as we shall see with the Easter Vigil. Whether the palm theme at Toledo originally replaced an older passion narrative at the Eucharist is impossible to say; but it is more 'historically' minded.

As circumstances vary today, so they did in the churches which used these old and varied liturgical books. For example, what was possible in the elaborate, urban context of Toledo would not have been appropriate in a small village in the south of France. If a book has only a simple palm blessing, this may well evidence local resources as much as conservatism. But the palm prelude elaborates in other ways. One is in the type of blessing. Most of these actually *bless* the branches, though there is one prayer which does not, and prefers instead to place the emphasis on the congregation's participation in the liturgical event. Another is in the thrust of the prayer itself; early tendencies bless the branches, whereas later ones add the theme of *protection* of the faithful. Similarly, while earlier prayers leave open the type of branch being used, later ones either specify palm, or allow for palm or olive. In Northern countries, prayers were sometimes adapted from their originals in order to permit local branches. Finally, in the Romano-Germanic Pontifical, the process of accumulation and elaboration resulted in the need to have a 'principal' blessing, to rank above others, and this was achieved by the device of prefixing the prayer with the solemn dialogue, 'Lift up your hearts'.

Other elaborations included additional readings (the Pontifical just mentioned had no less than four lections), a sermon, and a complicated procession. One can see the effect of architecture on these processions, since the grand basilican buildings of the Rhine afforded ample opportunity to make much of this day. The gospel book was usually carried at the head of the procession, but in the later Middle Ages, the cult of the sacrament left its own mark, for at Salisbury, the host was solemnly carried, being added to the procession after its beginning. The processional chants also elaborated and varied, according to local tradition. But there can be little doubt that in many places (not just cathedrals), the Palm Sunday liturgy was lengthy, and made considerable impact on the faithful.

It was doubtless as a result of its length, elaboration, and the popularity of the procession of the host that the Reformers got rid of the first part of the Palm Sunday liturgy altogether. In the old Prayer Book, all that remains (ironically) is a form of the older passion theme Eucharist, with nothing special about the day at all, except the length of the gospel. The Missal produced after the Council of Trent (that of 1570) simplified much of the medieval excesses, but still left several blessings, preceded by two lections. In the nineteenth century, Tractarian Missals either adopt the 1570 scheme or alter it slightly. The Catholic Apostolic rite, by contrast, has the palm gospel (Matt. 21.1-17) at the Eucharist itself, but it clothes the Eucharist with a penitential atmosphere.

In the 1928 Prayer Book, however, the palm gospel is allowed to be read at the Eucharist itself, 'when there are more celebrations of the Holy Communion than one'. Such an ominous provision is yet one more indication of the inability of many people to hold the two themes together, and the length of the service probably was part of such an attitude. But the 1930 *Directory of Ceremonial* will have none of this; a simplified form of the medieval Salisbury rite is recommended, with the palm lection from the Fourth Gospel (John 12.12-19 - a peculiarity of Sarum). Various options are suggested for the procession itself, and the Eucharist follows. The *Directory* also makes some suggestions for suitable music.

The Roman Catholic reforms in 1956 simplified the 1570 provisions considerably, so that the blessing of the palms is less complex, and the palm gospel is read immediately before the procession. The old hymn, attributed to Theodulf of Orleans, 'Gloria laus' (well known in the English translation, 'All glory, laud and honour') remains as the processional chant.

The 1970 Roman Missal keeps the traditional double theme of the day, which is reflected in the title. 'Dominica in palmis de passione domini' is indeed difficult to translate. English versions of this missal speak of 'Passion Sunday', but avoiding the palm theme does not solve the problem. A clumsy translation would be 'Palm Sunday of the Passion of the Lord'. The Roman revisers adapted the title from the old Gelasian Sacramentary, obviously not taking up the (almost universal) description of the day as of 'palms' in the various early medieval service books. Two new features occur in the rite which are in line with modern revisions as a whole. One is that the president 'introduces' the liturgy with a short explanation. Another is that the two gospel readings, both that of the palm and that of the passion, follow a three-year sequence, going through the synoptics. (The Johannine palm narrative gets in as an alternative to Mark, but the Johannine passion narrative is used exclusively on Good Friday.)

Unlike previous Roman books, the 1970 Missal allows for a 'solemn' and a 'simple' form for the palm rite, which is consistent with the way in which varied circumstances are officially recognized in modern Roman Catholic texts. The prayer over the palms precedes the gospel. Significantly, there is only one such prayer; the first alternative is a simple blessing, based on a traditional one; the second does not 'bless' the palms, but prays for the congregation (it is an adaptation of a prayer from the Romano-Germanic Pontifical). At the Eucharist, the passion narrative is read in traditional austerity, without incense, lights, or response. In earlier times, it was customary to symbolize the two aspects of this day in a change of liturgical colour, red for palms, purple for passion. Red has now taken over as the only colour for the entire liturgy.

The JLG proposals of 1971 and 1983 provide a simplified version of the Roman scheme, keeping the two themes as well as the two gospels. The prayers over the palms (1983 gives two alternatives) cleverly avoid 'blessing' the palms. The 1983 form suggests 'All glory, laud, and honour' as the processional hymn, and provides dramatic renderings for the passion gospels. Because of JLG's two-year cycle, only the Matthean and the Marcan palm gospels are provided, which is an impoverishment, because of the special character of the Lucan palm story.

The American Prayer Book (1979) begins with a collect (adapted from a Latin original) and reads the palm gospel (one

43

of the synoptics) *before* the solemn prayer over the palms. This latter begins with 'The Lord be with you' and 'Let us give thanks to the Lord our God', to give the prayer a special significance. It just avoids 'blessing' the palms!

One practical consequence of the kind of prayer used over the branches concerns the distribution. In previous times, the palms (or branches) were solemnly given to each person after the blessing. Nowadays, the tendency is to distribute them before the service begins, and this is reflected in all the modern revisions. Whatever kind of branch is used, there are no longer any special associations with 'protection' involved in the liturgy for this day, even though many people will keep their palm cross (if palms *are* used) in a special place through the ensuing year.

The new service

The new service suggests that the people bring branches with them to the liturgy from their homes. It takes a form similar to the new Roman Catholic rite, using its opening acclamation, and adapting its sample 'introduction' by the president. The prayer over the palms is a simplified version of the American Episcopal form. The lections for both the palm and the passion liturgies follow the new Roman scheme. A new feature is the special form of intercession, which is succinct and to the point, no doubt included in an attempt to ensure that intercession *is* offered on this day during such a long liturgy. In the interests of brevity, the sermon is optional, as is the Nicene Creed. It is, perhaps, a pity that the former should be regarded in this light, but it may well represent a healthy reaction against the wordiness of many modern services, particularly in explanatory material so often provided for the benefit of the faithful. (The prayers of penitence may also be omitted.) Two proper prefaces are provided, both already in ASB. The Roman preface for this day is a beautiful adaptation of an ancient form:

> Though innocent, he willingly gave his life for sinners;
> though guiltless, he suffered condemnation for the guilty.
> His death has wiped away our sins,
> his resurrection has reconciled us to you.

But each of these prefaces, in its own way, holds together the fullness of redemption which is the secret of the entire week's celebration. The Post-Communion is the ASB Collect for Lent 3, an inspired choice.

Palm Sunday combines a great deal. The new service has obviously benefited from the Roman, American Episcopal, and JLG revisions. It recommends a proper procession, starting perhaps in another building. It also emphasizes the fact that this procession is no piece of play-acting, no representation of Christ, as if suffering and death were to be left for another episode in the ensuing drama. Liturgical time is never a case of 'let's pretend'. Moreover, the prayer over the palms (or branches) captures this theme entirely when it ends:

> and follow him in the way that leads to eternal life.

Holy Week is about paradox.

And yet there are problems in fitting the whole liturgy together, which are raised by the question-marks over the sermon, the creed, even the intercessions and prayers of penitence. Many congregations will need some careful educating through this, and perhaps be helped into a more judicious use of options on ordinary Sundays, since in some churches, the ASB services are 'gone through' in a relentless fashion, with no attention paid to the principle of options themselves. Dramatic renderings of the passion gospel inevitably lengthen the service, yet mean a great measure of participation. Perhaps a *short* sermon, dwelling on *one* aspect of the day, is in order. Perhaps, too, the sample intercessions could be abbreviated, and inserted at the end of the eucharistic prayer; this would, of course, mean taking liberties which some would regard as improper.

Egeria, that modest 'matter-of-fact' nun, would be horrified had she known what careful attention was to be paid to her diary. But it provides us with a unique contribution to the history of liturgy, which is all the more important in that it is written in the style of a literate person who is not a specialist in liturgy! When we come to Holy Week itself, Lent reaches a particular peak, and thoughts go towards specific 'events' in the way of redemption, whereas previous to this stage, gospel lections have concentrated on Jesus' teaching, and his relation-ships with his followers. Holy Week, by contrast, involves bringing Jerusalem into the local congregation in a way that is not true of any other time in the Church's year. Sometimes, nowadays, fears of anti-Semitism rear up among Christians who lament past attitudes. But the little Syrian hymn quoted earlier christologizes the day perfectly. It is not *Jesus* against *Jews*. Rather, *Jesus* is confronting the *whole* of humanity, in particular, the Christian community. It is much easier to marginalize the whole experience into history, or even into an obsession with getting the liturgy clean and proper. What we need on this 'Palm Sunday of the Passion' is an atmosphere of divine realism, which avoids trivializing representations (in-cluding, even, those beloved donkeys), and cuts through human evasion, and reaches the heart of the matter in hand. For congregations which are used to being static during worship, the experience of walking together, in solidarity of purpose, may become a powerful (if occasionally embarrassing) means of focusing on the way to the cross.

Using the 1986 Service

Those who have followed the 1928 provision have grown used to the idea of giving two celebrations on this day a different feel, one emphasizing the palm story, the other the passion. It is clear, from what has already been written, and from the shape of the new service, that this is to be resisted. It is almost of the nature of this Sunday to hold palm and passion together at every celebration. No provision is made, therefore, for the use of the Palm Sunday story as the liturgical gospel in the customary place within the Eucharist; a passion narrative is always ordered, even if it sometimes has to be an abbreviated one.

This tension between two themes is not an historical accident or a liturgical nightmare, nor is it just a confusion of ideas, for within the service there is a definite movement from one to the other, with each half of the rite having its distinct, and almost opposite, ethos. It ensures that the faithful, who will in most cases not return until Maundy Thursday, will not take home with them only the carnival atmosphere of the procession of palms, but will have been led a little further along the path that Jesus walks through Holy Week, so that they return on Maundy Thursday attuned to the spirit of the Lord on that day. But it also ensures that those who will not, for one reason or other, be in church again for a full week, on Easter morning, will hear the full story of our redemption, instead of passing superficially from the joy of the King entering the city to the joy of the Lord who has overcome death.

The procession is integral to the service, at least at the principal service of the day. A procession is a religious movement which, wherever possible, people should *experience* rather than watch. Whenever it happens, it is a symbolic act of pilgrimage. Here, on Palm Sunday, it is an act that represents, and indeed helps to bring about, an identification with Christ as he goes to face his destiny. The procession should therefore never be reduced to something done by clergy, choir and servers alone. Let the people process! There are a number of possible starting places and the best one can only be chosen locally. There may be a daughter church, or the church of another denomination that is to share in the liturgy, or a nearby church hall. Or there may be a village green, playing field or shopping precinct. At the very least there may be a church gate and a pathway up to the church. In most circumstances the procession will not want to be very long, for it will not move very fast and there is a wealth of material to be used once it is over, little of which can be omitted without serious loss to the service, and a quarter of a mile may often be enough.

People and priest assemble at the starting point. If it is in the open air, care needs to be taken to ensure that all can understand what is happening and what is being said. An 'on-site' meeting beforehand with sidesmen, choir leader and others will be essential if the numbers expected to come are even moderately large. Amplification for marshalling instructions before the liturgy begins, and for the open air part of the service, will be desirable, but where this is not possible (though nowadays few congregations have nobody among their number without these skills and the equipment to go with it) a full text of

47

the service for everyone will enable all to follow even when they have to strain to hear.

The introduction to this section of *Lent, Holy Week, Easter* discusses quite fully the question of 'palms' and a note defines the word in such a way as to cover everything from branches of local trees to palm crosses. There is an encouragement to the idea that people bring their own 'branches' from the garden. Not everyone has a garden, so some branches will need to be provided. A palm procession is not a sort of historical reconstruction that calls for authentic Jewish palm. The point is that the people cut down the branches along the way, and so it is appropriate to use the foliage of trees found locally, whatever they may be, and in England in March or April that will often mean 'pussy willow' and forsythia. But palm crosses have a special place in the affection and devotion of many Anglicans and it would be foolish to deny these to those who value them. There is no reason why people should not have both - a branch of a good size, to carry in procession, and a palm cross, to take home as a reminder of the day and its liturgy.

The 1986 instructions are also quite clear that there is to be no liturgical distribution of the palms. Such a distribution would in any case be cumbersome for large numbers in the open air. But the objection is not just a practical one. A liturgical distribution puts the emphasis at the wrong point: it is not the receiving of a palm, but the carrying of one in honour of our Lord and his entry into Jerusalem that is significant. Where palms are to be provided by the church, rather than brought by the people, they may simply be given out with the service sheet or book.

The service at the starting point may be very short and simple. If it is outside, the anthems provided (at section 1) are more likely to be said than sung, and there then follow the greeting (section 2), a short introduction to set the scene, with a rather formal sample text provided (section 3) and a prayer over the palms, for which the people are instructed to hold up the palms. The palm gospel, which, unlike the passion gospel within the Eucharist itself, has the traditional acclamations at beginning and end, is an optional part of the rite, but it is difficult to see many circumstances in which it would make sense to omit it. It forms the biblical basis for what is to happen and refreshes in the minds of the hearers a story, of which they know the outline, but of which the detail is often forgotten. The minister then invites the procession to be on its way.

The procession is not principally an act of witness. If it turns out to be this, well and good, but that is not the primary aim, and in most places on a Sunday morning would, in any case, not be achievable. It is a religious action to enrich the experience of the participant, not the onlooker. Nor is it exclusively a procession *of the passion*, as many Good Friday processions have been. Of course there is that element of what is to come in Holy Week about it, and it is a following of Christ along a path that does lead to suffering and death, and certainly a cross will frequently head the procession. But it is a procession that majors on the triumphal entry, which was an occasion of festivity, joy and the celebration of kingship. There is a little bit of the atmosphere of carnival appropriate to this occasion, though it could degenerate to a point where little would be gained from it spiritually.

Because it is a joyful occasion, music and singing will be better than walking in silence. A band will be an enormous help, or, at very least, any choir needs to be placed in the *middle* of the procession, else all the sound will get lost 'up front'. 'All glory, laud and honour' is the obvious hymn, though there are others, and 'Lift high the cross' also has the virtue of an easy repeatable chorus. 'Ride on! ride on in majesty' is best kept to a little later (see below).

A degree of confusion is almost inevitable on such an occasion. Tidy Anglican minds cope with this only with difficulty, and indeed it is demanding of the sensitivity of both priest and people that there should be a semi-informal liturgical act, like this is bound to be, where boundaries cannot be clearly drawn between participants and spectators (boys on bicycles are known to join these processions!), nor between religious experience and simple human enjoyment. But it is possible to be reverent even when some chaos is inevitable.

What about the donkey? The tradition has had no place for

49

one and *Lent, Holy Week, Easter* does not so much as mention one. This is not just a sort of liturgical purism that will not stoop to the vulgar, in the best sense, and popular. Of course it cannot be wrong to have a donkey in the procession. But there are reasons to hesitate. One is simply that it comes to be the dominant symbol of the day and that people come for, or remember, not the experience of processing, or the carrying of branches, or the passion that is to follow, but the donkey, and that is to place the emphasis at the wrong point. There is also a deeper reason: it is to do with where we focus the presence of Christ in our procession. We do not have a Jesus-substitute dressed up, nor do we imagine the priest (who walks not rides) in that role. Christ is present in his Body the Church, the company of the faithful as they walk. A donkey disguises that either by focusing his presence, in the imagination of the people, on a donkey, or by suggesting, because the donkey is riderless, that in this reconstruction Christ is not actually present at all. The tradition is right to be wary of donkeys.

Though it may seem obvious, it is worth mentioning the need to have made wet-weather plans. People need to know what modifications are to be made to time, meeting place or service if it pours with rain. If the whole service has to be moved into the church, sections 1 to 5 may be used as they are written. What kind of procession can be contemplated indoors will depend on the building. It may be possible for all to weave their way around the church up and down aisles, it may be necessary to restrict the procession to a representative group (including all the children perhaps?) or the procession may have to be abandoned. But it does need to have been thought through in advance.

The end of the procession marks an important and dramatic moment of change and transition in the service. We move into the new atmosphere of the build up to the crucifixion. This will be expressed in the opening words of the Eucharist proper, the collect (section 8) which has no mention of palms or joyful crowds and moves straight to the heart of it all:

> Almighty and everlasting God,
> who in your tender love towards mankind

sent your Son our Saviour Jesus Christ
to take upon him our flesh
and to suffer death upon the cross . . .

That transition can often be made more effective by the use of a particular hymn. The people have reached the church, have left their branches outside (perhaps in a great heap that can become the bonfire for the Easter celebration) and have filed into the church and to their places, where any additional books will need to await them. When they are all ready, 'Ride on! ride on in majesty' is sung as the priest and other ministers approach the sanctuary. Though other hymns, psalms or anthems, might achieve the change in mood, it is difficult to think of one that will do it more effectively.

The Ministry of the Word now follows. Notes and rubrics urge the use of *all* the material provided - three lections, the last of them a full passion as well as the gradual psalm. It is difficult to see how this can be done within an average Parish Communion setting, but its desirability can be clearly seen, and omissions should be made sparingly. For many, the psalm (section 10) will be the first candidate for omission. This would be a pity, for these crucial verses of Psalm 69 (there is a selection of nine) ought to be heard and used by all the faithful in Holy Week. Since much of the usual material has been omitted from the beginning of the Eucharist, we have reached the gradual very quickly after the introit hymn, so there would be a stronger than usual argument for a psalm here, perhaps said rather than sung, rather than a hymn.

The passion reading, we have noted, is not, under any circumstances, to be omitted, though it may, if necessary, be abbreviated. There is an instruction to 'stand' and some will think it wrong for the members of the congregation to be seated for any of the passion, but, as a note concedes, it may be appropriate to have them seated until a dramatic moment (for instance, when he is led into Pilate's court) when they stand. Though there is an element of identification with our Lord in standing throughout, it is probably more important that the people be *receptive*, and those with aching feet for whom the

51

passion has become an endurance test may not be taking much in or be much moved by it.

The modern fashion is to increase beyond the traditional three the number of those taking part in the reading of the passion story, and, indeed *Lent, Holy Week, Easter* provides the texts set out for congregational oral participation, speaking the parts attributed to the crowd and other groups. It is certainly true that such participation allows people to enter much more fully into the events. For some this participation has brought the Holy Week story alive in a quite new way. There has, however, been some reserve expressed about this fashion and *Lent, Holy Week, Easter* does not urge it very forcibly. It is that the Christian is called in Holy Week to identify with *Christ*, not with all the other 'actors' in the drama, and that identification with Christ is expressed most aptly by a *silent* hearing of the passion, reflecting the silent acceptance of Christ. A decision has to be made locally, but these are the two sides of the argument to be weighed. One possible solution that has been found satisfactory is to read the passion on Palm Sunday with full congregational participation, to help create within the people the emotions of Holy Week, but to read it on Good Friday with representative readers and the congregation silent; for by that stage in the week they should have so identified with their Lord as not to want to shout 'Crucify!' as if they were the crowd.

The sermon (section 14) is, on this one Sunday, optional. In a sense, it has all been said in the reading of the passion. But there will sometimes be one simple point to be made briefly, but it will need to be sensitively composed if it is not to break the build up of passion material that continues into the eucharistic action. It may sometimes simply be an invitation to respond to the passion by a careful observance of the remaining days of Holy Week - in other words a form of 'giving out the notices', though other forms of notice would jar here. The creed (section 15) should almost certainly be omitted as superfluous in a service in which there is so much material that needs to be retained. The intercession prayers (section 16) relate directly to the passion theme and are penitential in character. They should certainly not be broken up by any interpolation of local material into the text. Local needs of overriding importance could be mentioned in a bidding at the beginning, but on this occasion the use of set text (framed especially for the day) is probably better than local material. The use at this point of the *Trisagion* (section 17) as a concluding congregational response is appropriate and rounds off an intercession that otherwise ends unconvincingly. The instruction to omit the Prayers of Penitence is right, but, at another level, misleading. For the usual penitential material is best omitted, simply because the whole rite has been penitential in character and in particular the intercession prayers have had a very distinctive penitential feel about them. The intercessions therefore lead into the Peace and then the Eucharist continues as usual. The note for Good Friday that recommends Eucharist Prayer 4 in Rite A might well also have been attached to Palm Sunday. Users of Rite B would similarly find it helpful to use the First Thanksgiving Prayer, even if this is not in regular use in their church.

What has been described here is clearly the order for the principal Eucharist of the day. What of the 'early service' tradition? It would seem that what is required is the same double theme of palm and passion, with sections 1-5 used before the Eucharist proper, which would then begin with the collect of the day and would include a passion gospel. Any attempt to opt for one theme and not the other, even at subsidiary services, is best resisted.

No provision is made in *Lent, Holy Week, Easter* for this service to be outside a eucharistic setting. Very few would fail to recognize the desirability of setting it within this context and so 'proclaiming the Lord's death until he comes'. Whatever the usual pattern in a church, Holy Communion should form part of the main service on this Sunday, if a priest is available. In his absence, this order could still be used up to section 17, with the collect at section 36 included in additional prayers to round it off, but it would be less satisfactory than the full rite, which provides a balanced and evocative beginning to Holy Week.

5 Maundy Thursday

Background

An evening Eucharist, with special commemoration of the Last Supper, is the almost universal custom of churches today. But this has not been the normal practice for Christians down the ages. For many people in antiquity, problems about fasting made an evening celebration difficult. For others, simply to attend (but not communicate) was sufficient. It is hard for us, who live in an age when evening celebrations are so popular, to understand the attitudes of other cultures to those things which we simply assume to be natural and correct.

However, the Maundy Thursday Eucharist, whenever it is celebrated on this day, has a meaning that is as rich and ambivalent as Palm Sunday. There is a little hymn (called a 'troparion') which is sung today in the Byzantine churches that encapsulates this rich two-sidedness:

> Receive me today, O Son of God, as a partaker of thy Mystic Feast;
> for I will not speak of the Mystery to thine enemies;
> I will not kiss thee as did Judas;
> but as the thief I will confess thee:
> Lord, remember me when thou comest in thy Kingdom.

This hymn is the chant which is sung both during the Great Entrance (the procession with the holy gifts) and at the Communion, and at the dismissal, on the 'Great and Holy Thursday' (as the Byzantines call it). It is supremely appropriate for the day, as it speaks humanly and penitently of the aspirations of ordinary Christians as they approach the holy table on this special occasion. Christians do not come to the altar on this Thursday as if the day stands on its own. Just as those who greet the Lord on Palm Sunday with 'Hosanna' know that 'Crucify him' is to be the louder cry later in the week, so on Thursday those who draw near with faith pray that they will be received into the Kingdom, in spite of their inability to understand fully the ways of God. So the attitude is that of the penitent thief, who confesses his wickedness, not that of the betrayer.

It is unusual to have such a hymn sung three times at a Byzantine Eucharist, *and* one that does not rely exclusively on psalmic sources. It may originally have been sung only at the communion. Evidence suggests that it was in use as early as the sixth century. Special material is, once more, required for a special occasion. Moreover, perhaps as a result of the devotional quality of its underlying sentiments, it helps to make up a longer prayer said by the president and the deacon just before communion at every celebration. Not surprisingly, this prayer dates from a much later stage in the evolution of the Byzantine liturgy, the fourteenth century.

Maundy Thursday looks back to previous enthusiasm for Christ and forward to betrayal and crucifixion. But what of the days leading up to it? The Monday, Tuesday, and Wednesday of Holy Week have been variously used down the ages. Egeria describes these days in some detail. Monday has a special service in the afternoon, and although she does not tell us which readings are used, a Lectionary from the following century has the story of the mother of the sons of Zebedee (Matt. 20. 17-28), which ends with a warning from Jesus about the cost of the Kingdom. On Tuesday, late in the evening, there is another special service, at the Anastasis, which concludes with the long reading of Matthew's farewell discourse (Matt. 24.1—26.2); this ends with the flat statement that the Son of Man is to be handed over to be crucified. Wednesday ends even more dramatically: the bishop goes into the cave of the Anastasis, while a presbyter reads a narrative of the betrayal of Jesus (Matt. 26.3-16), and Egeria adds:

> The people groan and lament at this reading
> in a way that would make you weep to hear them.

There does not seem to have been a daily Eucharist on these days, for it is only in the sixth and seventh centuries that the Latin West, the enthusiast for weekday Eucharists, incorporates this practice into Holy Week. And whereas Egeria's scheme lets Matthew's Gospel dominate the special readings on these days, in the West, there are lengthy lections from the Old Testament at the offices. For example, in Ambrose's time, the whole of Job was read on Monday at Milan. Eucharistic lectionaries have Old Testament readings, which is a sign of conservatism and antiquity.

But there are other features in these days which set them apart, to make them into a sort of limbo. In later centuries, bell-ringing is strictly forbidden (some would regard this as a blessed relief!); no elaborate music; feasts are to be transferred, so that they do not get in the way; even the office for the dead and requiem Masses are not unknown. Looking at such provisions in the Middle Ages, one is struck by the need to do something, in order to fill in time and add to the mood of sombreness.

We have already observed that the old Roman gospel readings at Mass were based on the passion narratives; Matthew on the Sunday, Mark on Tuesday, Luke on Wednesday, and John on Good Friday. Monday neatly had the story of the anointing of Jesus at Bethany (John 12.1-9). The Prayer Book altered some of these, but kept the basic rationale. On the other hand, the JLG proposals go for themes; penitence on Monday, obedience on Tuesday, service on Wednesdays; and the 1983 version supplies additional themes so that Monday is 'the day of cleansing', Tuesday is 'the day of teaching', and Wednesday is 'the day of waiting'. Tuesday's service of 'obedience' incorporates the Methodist renewal of covenant, and the 1983 version even adds a baptismal flavour to this rite. Services like these have the advantage of concentrating on one idea, which softens the blow for people who are not used to going to extra services on weekdays, even at this stage of the year. Themes, it could be suggested, are the educationalist's answer to 'representational' piety.

The Roman Missal (1970), on which many of the lections in the new services for this week are based, steps out in a different direction. Because the three synoptic passion narratives are to be read on alternate years at the Sunday Eucharist, and because the Fourth Gospel's passion narrative is reserved (by ancient tradition) for Good Friday, the compilers of this lectionary had to rethink the scheme. There are still no epistles, but Old Testament lections, from the servant songs of Isaiah, which is a happy blend of some old lectionaries and a nod to biblical scholarship. For the gospel readings, Monday keeps the anointing at Bethany, but Tuesday has the prophecy by Jesus that Peter will deny him (John 13.21-33, 36-8), and Wednesday now has the narrative of the betrayal (Matt. 26.14-25). Although the new services provide other options in its appended lectionary, these are the main eucharistic lections, and they take some beating for appropriateness to this week.

Moving back, now, to Maundy Thursday, we can see how it fits better into the entire scheme of Holy Week if it is built up to by some days of basic reflection on the meaning of Christ's death. Getting rid of those passion narratives, so that one of the Synoptics is read on the Sunday before, and John on Good Friday, means that weekday Eucharists are not unduly prolonged. A gentle 'historicism' through the use of the new gospels on Monday, Tuesday, and Wednesday will only serve to heighten the tension of Maundy Thursday. That is all for the good.

Special associations?

But Maundy Thursday itself, like so much of Holy Week, is a bit of a jumble of associations. In the Roman Missal (1970), the evening Eucharist is the start of the 'Triduum', and this feeling after a Christian 'Pasch', spread over three days, was *still* insisted upon during the time when Holy Week was evolving as a working backwards from the single, 'unitive' celebration of the Pasch on the Saturday night. However, the 'Triduum' was first identified with Good Friday, Holy Saturday, and Easter Day, rather than starting with Maundy Thursday evening. The new Roman calculation, though based on the same anxiety to hold together the central 'events', perhaps rings more truly to peoples' expectations, and biblical scholarship as well, since the 'Paschal Three Days' really begin with the institution of the Eucharist and end with Easter.

Two other relics of 'Passover' remain for this Thursday. One is that in the Syrian Church, it is still called the 'Pasch', even though Easter has long been central. Another lies in the origin of one of the customs associated with Maundy Thursday, the foot-washing, from which the English nick-name 'Maundy' is derived. Today, the British monarch distributes coins to select pensioners, which is a secular adaptation of the 'mandatum', the 'command' of Jesus, when he washed the feet of the disciples (John 13.1-15). There is some evidence to suggest that the reason for this practice was not through a desire to imitate Christ, but because footwashing was associated with the baptismal liturgy in some areas of the West, whether on Easter night or on this day. Thus, Ambrose inherited footwashing at Milan in the Easter liturgy, and he had to defend its use as a marked difference from Rome. It is also what Augustine found at Hippo, in North Africa, but on Maundy Thursday, as a practice to be undergone by those who were to be baptized at the Easter liturgy, though he allowed others to have their feet washed as well. According to this view, footwashing is part of the *mystery of sanctification*, rather than an *example of humility*. Both emphases are to be found in this acted parable. But it is the latter interpretation which takes over, as the footwashing becomes part of the Last Supper Eucharist, and is not restricted to baptism candidates, but is open to all.

In time, three special associations developed with this day, two of which were functional, the third obviously symbolic. The first stemmed from the need to reconcile those penitents who were due to rejoin the eucharistic fellowship in time for Easter. In some places, this took place on Good Friday, but at Rome, and in those churches which followed the Roman rite, this was done on the Thursday before Easter. Rites vary, but the basic outline recurs. The penitent comes forward before the offertory from the place reserved for him at the back of the church, and the deacon prays to the bishop on his behalf. The bishop warns the penitent not to repeat his sins. Three prayers follow, two collects and a lengthy absolution, which reconciled the penitent to the community. As time goes on, the rite is elaborated, and there is a tendency to add 'declaratory' absolutions to the earlier 'precatory' formulae. But from the fourth century, such public

58

reconciliation of penitents is restricted to the bishop, and this rule persisted in the West, right down to the Second Vatican Council, even though the actual celebration of public reconciliation was sporadic in recent centuries (it was the practice of several French dioceses in the eighteenth and early nineteenth centuries, in the heyday of 'Neo-Gallicanism'). There is no corresponding rite for this day in the new Roman Catholic service books.

The second special feature of this day concerns the preparation of oils for use at the baptismal liturgy during the Easter Vigil. It is a moot point as to when precisely oils came to be used at baptism. Certainly the practice was universal by the third century. And it appears that the oil (or oils, depending on how many anointings were given) was prepared and prayed over at the baptism itself. But preparation and blessing elaborated, hence the need to prepare and bless on a convenient occasion beforehand. Eventually, this resulted in the complex 'Mass of the Chrism', which has been reformed after Vatican II. Oil for the sick was included in this liturgy as a convenience. In the old Sacramentaries, the oil for the sick is blessed at the end of the eucharistic prayer; the oil of chrism and the oil of exorcism are blessed after communion. Before Vatican II, this was also the only Eucharist (apart from ordinations) at which concelebration was practised.

Although the 'Chrism Mass' (as it came to be called) does not appear in the new services, it is worth explaining briefly the new rite as it appears in the post-Vatican II books. Blessing oil was, like public reconciliation of penitents, restricted to the bishop, and when the new Missal was being prepared, Pope Paul VI was anxious that a 'priestly' element should be introduced into the new rite, together with an entirely new feature, the renewal of priestly vows. This explains why the three mass prayers for this service are altogether new. The blessing of the oils can either take place in the traditional positions, or else follow the renewal of priestly vows and lead into the offertory. The difference between Roman and Anglican practice with regard to anointing is that chrism is used in the Roman Catholic Church at ordination, hence the symbolic connection between the vows of presbyters and the blessing of this oil. For Anglicans, however, such anointing is not universal practice, although anointing the sick is (by contrast) on the increase. Some Anglicans, moreover, suspect these vow renewals (whether of ordination promises or those of baptism) as being one more manifestation of the self-conscious character of contemporary Christianity; and the priestly vows could even be identified as a reflection of disciplinary problems within the Roman Church in the 1960s. On the other hand, this new form of service (whether adapted or not) has become popular in many Anglican cathedrals, as it provides an occasion for clergy to get away from their local work at a busy time and meet their bishop.

The old Sacramentaries differ over whether these two tasks, of reconciling penitents and blessing oil, should have their own Masses, or whether they should be combined with the third (and symbolic) aspect of Maundy Thursday, the Last Supper Mass. The Western rite as a whole does have a genius for taking over a new custom and incorporating it into a Eucharist, as recent developments in the liturgical movement among all the churches have shown. Related to this question is also the matter of *when* the Last Supper Eucharist should be celebrated. For us, as we have observed, the evening is the most natural time of all. And yet such a Last Supper association does not appear central to Egeria's narrative, and there was not even an attempt, amidst all the 'holy geography' of Jerusalem in her time, to celebrate the eucharist where the Last Supper was supposed to have happened. She just notes, in passing, two celebrations, but they do not appear important.

The new service

But for us, it *is* important. It is hard for many today to imagine the impact of a late afternoon mass in a medieval village - the *only* occasion in the entire year when the Eucharist was celebrated in this way. Gradually, the time crept forward to the morning, but the earlier traditon (however it was actually observed) was to try to follow the chronology of the Gospels. Moreover, the custom of washing feet during the Eucharist brings its own piquant symbolism, and reflects the Church's traditional reliance on the Fourth Gospel as the 'spiritual' one. Washing feet, however, originally took place *after* Mass, and it was only in the 1956 revision of the Roman rite that it was incorporated within the body of the Eucharist, as was to happen with so many special features after Vatican II. It seems logical to us for the drama to follow immediately on the reading of the gospel, but not so in the Middle Ages. The old hymn, *Ubi Caritas*, was specially composed for the footwashing in a Benedictine community in Reichenau about AD 800, and it appears in the Roman Missal (1970) and the JLG texts (1971 and 1983) also provide for it.

For some, the footwashing is too uncomfortable, too real. For others, it is sublimely appropriate, especially if it follows a simple homily which does not try to 'explain' the symbolism (if symbolism needs explanation, then there is no point in having it). It is remarkable how in this century, the 'mandatum' has reached the heart of the Maundy Thursday Eucharist in so many traditions. The new service includes the footwashing, after the gospel (John 13.1-15 - the traditional reading), but (like the American Prayer Book) it does not suggest any special hymn, and this part of the rite may be concluded with a collect (that of Pentecost 11 in ASB, inspired by words from Augustine). Such a concluding device was employed of old when footwashing *followed* the Eucharist. The earlier part of the new rite begins with the prayers of penitence; these could be deemed inappropriate on this particular day. The Old Testament and epistle lections are from the new Roman service (and also JLG, Year 1). The new service also provides a special form of intercession, which reflects on Christ's teaching to his disciples (compare the special litany in the Lenten Service of Penitence, Form B). In order to recreate the atmosphere of the Last Supper, a special introduction is provided at the preparation of the gifts (JLG suggests the reading of the 'warrant' for the Eucharist, following Reformed tradition - 1 Cor. 11.23-9). The conclusion of the service brings us to two traditional features which are interrelated, but distinct in original function.

The first is the question of communion on Good Friday. In

61

the East and medieval West, and at Rome today, Good Friday is an 'aliturgic' day, i.e. a day on which the Eucharist is not celebrated. As we shall see in the next section, the desire arose for communion from the reserved sacrament on Good Friday, hence the need to take the consecrated species to a safe place. In the later Middle Ages, even though only the president received communion on Good Friday, a great deal of fuss was made of this transfer, and it became an elaborate procession, to and from a special altar. From the twelfth century onwards, the procession became a special feature of the end of Mass, and the practice of stripping the main altar (and the other altars of the church) only served to heighten the atmosphere of bareness. Some Anglicans have reintroduced this custom, and the new service allows for it in oblique references. Other Anglicans resist such an innovation, with its overtones of medievalism and the 'cult of the sacrament'. Others again understand its origin but do not see its appropriateness within the context of a renewed liturgy.

The second traditional feature is the 'Watch'. Egeria noted a lengthy series of services at Gethsemane, with readings about Jesus' watch in prayer. The Romano-Germanic Pontifical has a long sequence of readings from the Fourth Gospel, corresponding to those lections (John 13.16—17.26), and these occur during the footwashing, which follows Mass. The Catholic Apostolic rite (nineteenth century) has similar readings, but after the simple transfer of the consecrated gifts to the sacristy at the end of the Eucharist (no footwashing). The new services provide for a synoptic 'Gospel of the Watch', and this may be preceded by an alternative series of readings (like those in the Pontifical just mentioned) from John 13.16—17.26, interspersed with suitable psalms, and silences.

There are many ways of performing this evening Eucharist. It is such an entity in itself that it would only be confused and atrophied if the blessing of oils were combined with it, as it was in many medieval (and post-medieval) Latin rites. To extend the Eucharist both by a special atmosphere (Last Supper), a special ceremony (the footwashing), and special reading (the Watch) is an important way of starting the 'Triduum Sacrum Paschale' or

'Holy Paschal Three Days'. The introductory notes to the new service imply as much when they speak of Thursday to Easter morning as a 'continuum'. In a time when evening celebrations are so common, it is doubly important that this Eucharist does not become yet one more in the regular diet. It should retain its special characteristics. For this reason, the sentiments of the first Post-Communion Prayer (which speaks of the heavenly banquet) are fundamental to the occasion, as are the Johannine lections at the Watch, which end with the high priestly prayer of Christ, wherein Jesus prays for the unity of his disciples.

Agape

The new services also provide for the celebration of the Eucharist during an ordinary meal, with the suggestion that such a rite may be appropriate for the earlier days of Holy Week, or it may even replace the more formal liturgy just described on Maundy Thursday. Many congregations find such 'agape'-celebrations a helpful way of recapturing the domestic background of the Eucharist. There does not appear to be any ancient precedent for such a service as a special feature for this stage of the liturgical year, although that is not necessarily an argument against the custom. Above all, however, Maundy Thursday is not a day for divisions among the community (of whatever kind) to surface, for it could well be that the demise of the agape in antiquity was due to its effect on the varied social groupings within many Christian congregations.

For some the experience of an agape of the sort described in *Lent, Holy Week, Easter* has brought the Last Supper alive, both in bringing out its passover overtones and in heightening the experience of fellowship. That is well and good, but the problem with setting the Maundy Thursday Eucharist within such a meal is that these are only two of the special features of the day and, indeed, to go home without being drawn into the experience of desolation that the stripping of the altar and the watch typify is to lose out on a very powerful part of the unfolding drama. Where Eucharist and agape are combined on this day, at least all should move into the church, if the agape

63

has been held elsewhere, to keep watch, rather than let the evening end in idle chatter like the average supper party.

There is a respectable school of scholarship that maintains (in this area of few records and much speculation) that, from the beginning, Eucharist and agape were always separate and different exercises, and for good reason, and that they are best kept separate today. In deference to this view, the suggestions provide not only for an integrated Eucharist-agape, but for a meal *after* the eucharistic celebration.

There are ideas in this section for fruitful experiment in many places and the note of caution sounded here is not, in the main, about the concept of an agape-Eucharist, but about its suitability to Maundy Thursday. It might be wise to use this form in Lent, or early in Holy Week, before ever considering its use for the Eucharist of the Last Supper, when it is desirable both that all the distinctive elements of the first Maundy Thursday find their place and also that all the Christian family in each community feel able to participate happily in what will usually be the only celebration of the day.

Using the 1986 Service

Tradition points to just one Eucharist in a church on Maundy Thursday (except, in some places, for the quite different 'Chrism Mass') and it would now be all but universally agreed that this should be in the evening, at the supposed hour of the 'supper' in the upper room. Although it is clear why one single celebration for the whole community is desirable, pastorally the priest may often see the need for an earlier celebration also, whether for the elderly who do not like to go out at night, or for parents with small children who will not both be able to come in the evening. Where this is the case, a mid- or late-afternoon celebration may capture the spirit of the occasion more than a morning one.

But, to turn to the main celebration, a service that will most appropriately begin in daylight and end in darkness, it is important on this night to maintain a balance between the special and the ordinary. Maundy Thursday evening illuminates every Eucharist and must therefore be recognizably 'what we always do'. If, in the interests of trying to create an authentic 'last supper', it doesn't feel like the regular celebration, an important connection will have been lost. If, on the other hand, it is *just* like any other evening celebration, the distinct richness of this night will have been denied to the people. The 1986 text has kept that balance and those who follow it sensitively will achieve it too.

There is another balance to be kept, as well as that between the special and the ordinary. Like Palm Sunday, Maundy Thursday is a subtle blend of two elements, both of which are present throughout, though one dominates until the other takes over. On Palm Sunday it was the balance between joy in the victorious King and sorrow at the onset of the passion, with the entry into the church at the end of the procession as the movement from the predominance of the first to the predominance of the second. On Maundy Thursday it is the balance between, on the one hand, the joy of fellowship with the Lord in the Eucharist and thanksgiving for it as a gift in which his presence is experienced and, on the other hand, the gathering gloom as the supper gives way to the Gethsemane agony and the arrest, with the prayer after communion as the turning point.

The service begins with an entrance song (section 1) and a greeting (section 2) that, right at the beginning, emphasizes the fellowship that is particularly strong in this celebration. The Prayers of Penitence (sections 3–7) have distinct features; a note indicates that they may be omitted where the footwashing is to take place. The *Gloria* (section 8) is sung or said, despite its omission through the penitential season of Lent, and its inclusion at this point on Maundy Thursday helps to create the restrained festivity of the day. The collect differs from that in ASB which provides two beautiful prayers, both better employed later in the service at sections 16 and 35.

The Ministry of the Word is straightforward. If one reading has to be omitted (and it is less easy on Maundy Thursday evening to see why this should be necessary), the Old Testament passage is less crucial than the epistle reading. The anthem at section 13 needs to be set to music, though, for those at home with its style, there is a musical version of precisely this text in *Sound of Living Waters*. Where the washing of the feet is to be observed, the sermon (section 15) needs to be of such a sort that it leads naturally into it. The theme has already been introduced in the gospel reading (section 14).

The washing of feet has not yet become as common in Anglican practice as some of the other special observances of Holy Week and Easter. It is not difficult to guess the reason. This is not a tidy ritual, nor one that can be made wholly elegant. Water, feet and the priest on his knees before his people doesn't fit easily into most people's idea of Anglican ceremonial, and the more solemn you try to make it to compensate, the more farcical it could become. But those who have taken the plunge, so to speak, would nearly all urge on their fellow Christians that they do include this in their liturgy on Maundy Thursday. Ritual is nearly always more fruitful for those who participate in it than for those who merely observe it. Each year the priest is given a marvellously humbling, yet uplifting, experience as he kneels to minister to his people, and each year twelve different people in his congregation are given the experience, as marvellously humbling, yet uplifting, of receiving his ministry in this way. It is worth it for what it does for thirteen people each year, however little it may do for the observers, though they do very often catch the atmosphere too. And if it isn't tidy and elegant, perhaps there's a lesson to be learned in that too!

Although twelve is, for an obvious reason, the usual number, it would be better to wash less than be so cramped in chancel or sanctuary that some effectiveness was lost. Nor, despite the Roman Missal, is it necessary for them all to be *men*. This is not just an historical reconstruction, but an acting out of relationships within the local church today in which there will be men, women and children. A fairly representative group is needed, if the whole message is to be received. (But, with women, warn them against tights!)

Jesus 'laid aside his garments'. Where the tradition is for the president to wear a chasuble, he might well 'lay it aside' as he, and other ministers (preferably those, whether ordained or lay, who share with him a position of authority and leadership in the

66

church community, rather than simply the usual servers) take bowl, jug and towel and go to each of those whose foot (one foot will do) is to be washed as they sit in places where they may be seen. Each footwashing must come over as a warm and human action of affection and service, not as a rather clinical liturgical ceremony. The president may well speak a brief word with each person or greet them with a handclasp, as at the Peace, if that helps to make it feel natural. The service notes for Maundy Thursday suggest a 'symbolic' wiping of the feet by a 'touch', rather than a proper wiping of them dry, but, especially if there are assistant ministers, it would be better that the job was done thoroughly by one of them! The same note speaks only of bowl and towel. The Gospel speaks of Jesus pouring water into a basin, and the action of pouring would seem to heighten the ceremony - else the congregation might even envisage an empty bowl.

Section 16 of the service allows this all to happen in silence, or during the singing of a hymn, an anthem or a psalm. An earlier note suggests Psalm 40 or the anthem *Ubi caritas* ('Where true love is'). This would certainly be a welcome addition to the repertoire of music in many churches, and not simply for use on Maundy Thursday. James Quinn has provided an excellent paraphrase of it ('God is love and where true love is, God himself is there'); and Brian Wren has written a beautiful hymn which takes the footwashing as its basic inspiration ('Lord God, your love has called us here'). When the washing of the feet has been completed, but probably before all return to their places, a collect (section 16, with an alternative noted) may be said, and it does indeed round off a section that would otherwise end rather indecisively.

The prayers of intercession (section 17) are particular to this night. Unlike those of Palm Sunday, they do allow for the interpolation of local material and specific petitions within their framework, but the style is terse and precise and any additions need to follow that style if the shape of the prayer is not to be lost. The prayer that follows (section 18) is, by contrast, in a richer and more florid style that moves the service on towards the commemoration of the Last Supper itself. It is

67

the form of the 'Prayer of Humble Access' that is found in the Rite A appendix and deserves to be better known, though, as always, there is a case for moving straight from intercession to the Peace.

Of late, liturgical scholarship has deprecated the use of any, and certainly, many words at the time of the preparation of the gifts, preferring to save all praise and prayer for the Eucharistic Prayer itself. But on this occasion special material is provided for this stage in the liturgy to bring out the passover origins of the Eucharist and, to an extent, to employ words our Lord himself may have used if this was indeed the passover meal (and about that point there is not, of course, unanimity). A note, easily missed, also invites the president, as he says the Eucharistic Prayer, to substitute for the words 'who in the same night that he was betrayed' words that underline the identification of this Eucharist with the first Maundy Thursday: 'who in *this* night when he was betrayed'. This is well phrased, for at all costs the unpleasing modification that some will have heard, 'who in the same night that he was betrayed, *that is, tonight*', is to be avoided.

Once the distribution of Holy Communion is over, the transition point is reached where the upper room must give way to the Garden of Gethsemane. Before people go to their homes, they must be drawn further along the path of this night's story and not be left in the comparative security of the Last Supper. The sense that it is night and that the darkness is coming down must be shared if, returning next day on Good Friday, the congregation is not to feel that they have missed out on a vital stage in an unfolding drama. Whether this change in mood is to be expressed quite briefly or developed through an extended watch has to be considered carefully, and what is done tonight in each place will depend in part on what it is planned to do on Good Friday. But, before examining the possibilities, it is important to emphasize that a 'watch' does not have to be before the consecrated elements and therefore need not be part of Holy Week only for those churches where the reservation of the sacrament or 'an altar of repose' is customary. A watch in a darkened church before a bare table in a church of a quite different tradition could be very helpful to many. But among the options that this part of the service provides, sight must not be lost of this basic need to take the faithful further along the path of identification with Christ through the events of this week and, in particular, through the agony of the garden and the pain of denial and desertion.

The minimal ending provided for the service is sentence, silence, one of two alternative collects and a dismissal (sections 31-6). There is no text for the congregation except an *Amen*. The collect is said by the president alone and the Dismissal ('Christ was obedient unto death. Go in his peace.') elicits no response; there is no blessing. These give the end of the service the necessary different feel. But the dismissal is a poor substitute for the watch, which, though it may be short, should be included wherever possible.

In planning a watch, it will be important to keep clear the two types of watch possible and the two orders for its observance. The first type is a *communal* watch, probably short, in which all (or most) of the congregation at the Eucharist participate together before going home. The second type is a *successive* watch, rather longer, where people keep watch in turn, perhaps on a predetermined rota, with just two or three at a time, returning to the church at some time in the evening or the night to take their 'turn'.

The two orders, about which more will be said, vary the position of the Gethsemane account ('The Gospel of the Watch'). The first order places it at the end of a cycle of readings, psalms and silence, where it becomes the *conclusion* of the watch. The second order places it at the *beginning* of a completely silent watch. Or the gospel of the watch may itself be divided paragraph by paragraph and read at points through the watch with silence in between. Confusion about either type or order will make for unsatisfactory planning.

The rubrics begin the watch with reference to a procession. Where a chapel is to be the setting for the watch, where the sacramental elements are to be the focus for that watch, and where consecrated bread (and wine) are to be kept for Holy Communion on Good Friday, this procession is, of course, to convey these elements to the chapel. For some Anglicans such an idea is quite foreign; for others it is quite familiar.

There may, of course, be need for movement to a side chapel for the watch even when there is no reservation. It depends very much on which sort of watch is envisaged. If it is to be a brief watch (the notes suggest a minimum of an hour), with as many of the congregation as possible encouraged to stay throughout, the watch will probably be at the altar of the celebration, unless there is a very large chapel. But, if it is to be a long watch through the night, with people coming and going, a silent procession to a chapel where a few may gather to pray will be appropriate. In any case the movement itself will help to accentuate the transition from upper room to garden, and from fellowship to isolation.

The rubric here refers to the possibility of a hymn or psalm. Those who transfer the consecrated elements at this point in the service will probably choose to use the great Thomas Aquinas' hymn 'Now, my tongue, the mystery telling'. But this hymn deserves a place in the celebration on Maundy Thursday night in all churches, and not just those with such a procession.

> That last night, at supper lying,
> 'Mid the Twelve, his chosen band . . .

Whether at the Preparation of the Gifts or after communion, it ought to be included. There is also a strong case, after communion, for singing Cardinal Newman's 'Praise to the holiest in the height', omitting the usual repeat of the first verse at the end, and so concluding the hymn

> And in the garden secretly,
> And on the Cross on high,
> Should teach his brethren, and inspire
> To suffer and to die.

It is an almost perfect lead in to the watch.

The essence of the watch is silence. It is a response to Christ's invitation to his disciples to watch with him. The Christian tries to identify with Christ in his loneliness and to share in his passion. A series of readings (taking us through the Johannine discourses) and psalms (the *Hallel* psalms of the passover festival) are provided. These will only be appropriate during a long watch of several hours, for the words should never do more than stimulate the silence into reflection and prayer; they should not ever replace the silence as the chief ingredient.

For the silence, many people will appreciate help with how best to use this time prayerfully. Especially if the second approach is being adopted, with complete silence rather than the Johannine discourses, it will be helpful to provide a sheet or card with words for prayer and reflection. Some of the material from 'Prayers on the Passion' in *Lent, Holy Week, Easter* would be useful.

The length and style of the watch – whether all together for a short time or a few at a time over many hours – will obviously affect the place of the 'ministers' within such a watch. If it is to be a short communal watch, the president and other clergy and the servers could well kneel at a step before the altar leading the people, either straightaway after the Eucharist without returning to the vestry at all, or after returning from the vestry where they have removed vestments etc.; the sense of the community in watch and prayer is strengthened by their presence there. But, naturally, when there is to be a much longer watch, the ministers will have to leave the sanctuary either before the watch begins or at a point soon after, returning individually as and when they choose.

The other element in the liturgy of this night is the stripping of the altar. The notes in *Lent, Holy Week, Easter* allow for the coverings to be removed and the lights extinguished during or immediately after the gospel of the watch or the reading of John 17, or, of course, during a psalm or hymn. This stripping of the altar, which seems to represent the desertion of Christ and the desolation of that night, as much as it does his stripping for crucifixion, is an appropriate response to the Gethsemane story. It must be simple, unhurried and unfussy to be effective. The candles are extinguished (and other lights may be put out gradually too), the vessels and other material from the Eucharist removed, the coverings of the altar table taken off and carried away, so that the sanctuary is left stark and bare. Where

71

there has been a procession to a chapel for a watch, the stripping will be unobserved by those who have gone to keep watch there, but, where the watch is at the altar of the eucharistic celebration, all may be drawn deeper into the Gethsemane experience by witnessing it. If it is to be part of the public liturgy, it should be carefully rehearsed. Nothing in the liturgical year requires more sensitivity of the participants than this: the slightest hint of hurry or fussiness at this point can completely spoil the service.

The note allows the stripping *during* the reading or *after* it. If the reading and the action are simultaneous, some of the biblical story, the aural impact, may be lost if the people are completely absorbed in the visual drama. It is probably safer when the one follows the other. Experience suggests that a public stripping of the altar is better provided with a musical background than left in silence. Psalm 54 is indicated, though it is suggested *before* the Gethsemane gospel. Psalm 69.1-22 is particularly suitable; only selected verses of it have been used on Palm Sunday. Psalm 22 is now part of the Good Friday service and therefore its traditional use on this night should probably cease. Where the focus has moved to a side chapel for the watch, the stripping is, of course, best done in silence. It should not distract from the watch.

6   Good Friday

Meaning

My people, what have I done to you?
How have I offended you? Answer me!

I led you out of Egypt, from slavery to freedom,
but you led your Saviour to the cross.

Holy is God! Holy and strong! Holy immortal one,
have mercy on us!

The old medieval Good Friday liturgy is made up of a number of strange elements, at the heart of which lies the veneration of the cross. During this rite, hymns of devotion are usually sung, and the most traditional is this painful cry of 'reproach' to the people of God. Never intended to be anti-Semitic, the 'Reproaches' (as they are called) probably come from the old Spanish church, which used Micah 6. 1-8 (v. 3 makes up the opening reproach, 'My people, what have I done to you?') on Good Friday. Something resembling them appears to have been used at Jerusalem. Then, in the later ninth century, an Antiphonal from Senlis, in France, put the first part of the hymn (as we now know it) together, with the *Trisagion* ('Holy is God . . .') plea for mercy, which was part of the old French and Spanish eucharistic rites on ordinary Sundays.

There is something dynamically Christian and thoroughly unsentimental about this chant. *Why* did you do it? Couldn't you *see* how futile it was? Sometimes it takes a persecuted people to see the full implications of this truth. Guido Rocha, a Brazilian artist, sculpted 'The Tortured Christ' in 1975, depicting the death-cry of Jesus in agony on the cross, and thereby expressed the strength of the Latin American church, although he himself would not formally describe himself as a Christian. Beneath the sculpture, Rocha comes right to the heart of the matter in an inscription: 'The characteristic of

Christ is that his life was totally coherent, so coherent that the world could not stand him.' With Christianity - and often when described by the 'outsider' - we are so frequently dealing with paradox.

The cross has long fascinated people, and it even knows non-Christian uses. The slaughtered passover lamb was placed on two platters, in the form of a cross. The cross was a means of ignominious crucifixion, and (of course) a more than usually horrible death. And it is from these two backgrounds that Christianity gains a symbol which it virtually monopolizes. There can be no Christian faith without the cross, and it haunts even actors who take the part of Christ in commercial films. Even in two thousand years, the dramatic and artistic potential of the cross has not been exhausted. However, history continues to surprise us; the early Christians, for all that many experienced martyrdom, had little use in depicting the cross, preferring instead symbols of resurrection. It is not until the fourth century and after that Christians went in for depicting the cross on a grand scale. Tradition has it that Elena, the Emperor Constantine's mother, 'found' the 'true' cross at Golgotha in 335, and we shall see later how the ritual veneration of the cross originated in the Jerusalem liturgy.

Similarly, in the sixth century, the Latin hymn-writer, Venantius Fortunatus made his most famous composition, *Vexilla regis prodeunt* ('The royal banners forward go'), which mixes the imagery of kingship with the facts of betrayal, crucifixion, and death. That hymn also meditates on the saving power of the 'Tree' of crucifixion, which is paralleled in an old Irish devotional prayer:

> O King of the Friday
> Whose limbs were stretched on the cross,
> O Lord who did suffer
> The bruises, the wounds, the loss,
> We stretch ourselves
> Beneath the shield of thy might,
> Some fruit from the tree of thy passion
> Fall on us this night!

Veneration of the cross (one might say) is *the* centre of Christianity. The actual rite of veneration is first described by Egeria at Jerusalem, though its origin in piety may well lie in the tradition of Christians praying to Christ as the crucified one who will return in glory from the east. Such was the early Syriac piety of domestic prayer, so that when the cross was 'found' by the Emperor's mother, the groundwork for the custom which Egeria describes on Good Friday was already firmly built. Popular piety so often brings together realities which theology tries to separate, in this case, the power of the saving cross, death and resurrection, incarnation and 'coming'.

All this means that our celebration of Good Friday can never degenerate into being a religious routine, in which we come together to mope, and to feel sorry for Jesus. In the churches which use the Good Friday liturgy contained in these new services, many pieties and theological emphases are likely to coexist, whether in the churchmanship of the congregation, or the religious experiences of individual worshippers. It may well be a mixture of, say, the agonized Christ of that Brazilian sculptor; the stylized Christ who hangs in shame against a divine, golden background in Eastern iconography; the Romanesque Christ who stands, fully clad, combining suffering and glory; the later medieval tendency to bring contemporary characters and problems into the whole passion drama; the stark figure of Reformation traditions, which stress the atoning sacrifice. The options continue to be open and the odds are that both within and outside the community of faith, that symbol, with its saving criminal on it, will fascinate the creative forces of human beings for a long time to come. Hymnody, too, provides many examples. Venantius Fortunatus wrote when the Roman Empire had crumbled. So, much later, Paul Gerhardt's 'O Haupt voll Blut und Wunden' ('O sacred head, surrounded') brings the suffering Christ into the context of the Thirty Years War in seventeenth-century Germany.

Suffering is easier to discuss than it is to redeem, and in our century, which has known the holocaust of Jewish massacres, and lives with high unemployment, and a frustrated utilitarianism in the background to many people's lives, it is too easy to be bland about God 'sending suffering', so that the Christian arrives on the scene to dole out the cross as if it is a divine blank cheque which covers the cost of all the pain and inconvenience and nausea which many of us have to face, either in daily life or in news bulletins. There is a lot of suffering which *need* not happen. There is a lot of suffering which *must* happen. Perhaps if Christians were prepared to suffer more, then other kinds of suffering which are unnecessary could be dealt with, and avoided. Yet all this should not lead us into making Good Friday an orgy of self-pity. It should, instead, help us come before God to purge ourselves of inessentials, so that we are ready to present ourselves as a living sacrifice (Rom. 12.1), anticipating a discipleship that will be costly. Good Friday is a day of *celebration* and *intercession*, which is why both these features dominate the traditional liturgy.

The Cross

Egeria's account of the Jerusalem liturgy continues through the early hours of Friday morning. There is a series of processional services which ends in a walk into the city to the main church, at the point where the crucifixion is supposed to have taken place, Golgotha; here, the account of the trial before Pilate is read (John 18.28—19.16). The bishop then sends the people home for some sleep, since (as Egeria notes) 'they have been hard at it all night, and there is further effort in store for them in the day ahead'.

The congregation reassembles at 8.00 a.m., when the 'holy wood of the cross' (the relic of the true cross) occupies the central place in a special and solemn liturgy. Egeria continues:

> The bishop's chair is placed on Golgotha . . . A table is placed before him with a cloth on it, the deacons stand round, and there is brought to him a gold and silver box containing the holy Wood of the Cross. It is opened, and the Wood of the Cross and the Title are taken out and placed on the table.
>
> As long as the holy Wood is on the table, the bishop sits with his hands resting on either end of it and holds it down, and the deacons

round him keep watch over it. They guard it like this because what happens now is that all the people, catechumens as well as faithful, come up one by one to the table. They stoop down over it, kiss the Wood, and move on. But on one occasion (I don't know when) one of them bit off a piece of the holy Wood and stole it away, and for this reason the deacons stand round and keep watch in case anyone dares to do the same again. Thus all the people go past one by one. They stoop down, touch the holy Wood first with their forehead and then with their eyes, and then kiss it, but no one puts out his hand to touch it.

This local ceremony goes on until midday, which means that it lasts a few hours. It is not a formal liturgy, for there are no hymns or chants or readings. But the act of veneration is placed within a context, because the people have been going to various services and will be attending even more. Egeria's account, however, gives no suggestion of stylization, so that though the ceremony is august, it is also somewhat informal.

When this is over, there is a long service which lasts the three hours, which is made up of readings, both of psalms, epistles, and gospels, all concerned with the sufferings of Christ; Egeria hints that one of the Old Testament lections was one which is nowadays called the 'suffering servant' (Isa. 52, 53). She is clearly struck by the intense atmosphere. At three o'clock, the account of Jesus' death is read (probably John 19.17-37). The day ends with a service which commemorates the burial of Christ, at the tomb.

Later Jerusalem liturgies build on these foundations. Strangely, the 'veneration' drops out altogether, and the three hours' service of readings expands considerably. In the evening, there is the 'burial' of the cross at vespers, and the liturgy of the presanctified, which has been celebrated regularly in Lent, except on Saturdays or Sundays (when the full liturgy is allowed).

Two words of explanation are in order here. The first is that Egeria does not use the word 'venerate'. That belongs to later, Western terminology, though in the later Middle Ages, the rite was frequently called 'Creeping to the Cross' in England. The word 'venerate' does, however, occur in a Byzantine hymn on Good Friday. But the terminology is fluid, which may explain why the new services opt for the term 'Proclamation of the Cross'. Secondly, the practice of receiving communion from the reserved sacrament, which became popular at Rome in the seventh century, may well have come from the East, in the Jerusalem practice alluded to earlier. But it does not belong to the original liturgy, and would seem (even in the East) to have been a provision for the very devout, since it, too, drops out of Eastern practice later on. We know that holy men and women kept supplies of consecrated Eucharist in their homes, so that they were able to communicate. But there is never any question, in antiquity, of celebrating the Eucharist on this day. On the other hand, we have already seen how (comparatively) late is the development of a popular Last Supper Eucharist on the preceding day. Perhaps the deep corporate memory of these holy days can only fix on one Eucharist, one paschal celebration, as the culmination of all these offices and rites, at dawn on Easter day.

The new services provide a rich and at the same time austere adaptation of all of this, based on the Roman Missal (1970), and the adaptations which are found both in the JLG books (1971 and 1983), the American Prayer Book (1979), and the liturgies of the Taizé community. The Roman form builds on earlier practice, and comes in four parts; the liturgy of the word, the solemn prayers, the veneration of the cross, and the communion. This old logic works through Scripture, intercession, and the cross, to receiving communion from the reserved sacrament in public, which is nowadays (and when the custom began at Rome) a very unusual practice. Anton Baumstark, who is really the founder of liturgy as a science in its own right, wrote earlier this century that liturgy is most conservative and resistant to change on special occasions. Good Friday proves him altogether correct, because in the first two parts of the old Roman liturgy, the readings and intercessions, we see the primitive form of the Roman liturgy of the word at every celebration of the Eucharist. It begins simply, without any preliminary prayers. It contains an Old Testament reading as well as an epistle. There is no creed.

After the homily, there are intercessions, which are made up of a series of biddings and collects, each in sequence, matching a particular topic for prayer.

Liturgy is not just a matter of history for its own sake. Many of the traditional features of Holy Week are deeply embedded in the way the special Jerusalem rites were adapted by the Western churches in the early Middle Ages. But in the case of this early Good Friday liturgy at Rome, we have clear evidence of a form of service which is simple and austere, whose simplicity and austerity persisted long after the regular celebration of the Eucharist developed extra prayers (at the start of Mass, as well as at other points), and lost other features (including the prayers of intercession themselves, whose traditional name is the 'prayer of the faithful'). Special occasions can save old items, and keep them in store for a time when Christian churches either need a refit for their liturgy (as with Roman Catholics after Vatican II) or can appropriate for themselves traditional features which were obscured by the time of the Reformation and therefore lost altogether under reforming zeal (Anglicans and others).

The new service

The new service, however, inverts the Roman order in an important way. The Word, rightly, begins the liturgy for Good Friday, and the communion may end it. But the 'Proclamation of the Cross' (as it is called) comes immediately after the Word, so that the intercessions follow it, and lead into communion (if there is to be one). The compilers of this service have opted for the structure which has long been known in the West at Milan, for the Ambrosian rite has often gone its own way, either in developing its own variations, or in maintaining its own independence as a matter of right (as was the case after the Council of Trent). The Ambrosian tradition, therefore, has the Word, followed by the veneration of the cross, followed by the solemn prayers of intercession. However, the Ambrosian rite never had the rite of communion, so that its threefold shape leads from Word to cross, as a liturgical climax, and then moves down in atmosphere to the intercessions. Arguably, the new service fits better into the historical scheme as well as developing its own dramatic form when there is no communion. However, the new service can be celebrated using the traditional Roman structure of Word, intercession, cross, and communion. Once again, variation of shape is apparent.

The Ministry of the Word begins with the direction that the ministers enter in silence. This is an old Roman custom, and it is intended to convey a sense of emptiness in a dramatic manner. The liturgy begins with a collect, from the JLG (1983) proposals; this prayer is an adaptation of the first 1662 collect. The Old Testament lection follows, again in the Roman tradition (Isa. 52.12—53. end - the 'suffering servant'). By long association, Ps.22 (but only vv. 1-22) comes between Old Testament and epistle. The second reading is a matter of choice (unlike the Roman liturgy, which directs a pericope which is the first of the three alternatives in the new service, Heb. 4.14-16; 5.7-9). The passion gospel consists of the Johannine narrative (John 18 and 19), again by long tradition. The 'suffering servant' is universally popular nowadays, although in antiquity it appears only in the old Spanish lectionary. This Word-liturgy is quite unlike its Roman predecessor, because it reads in a manner similar to a simplified Word-liturgy from the ASB, so that its austerity does not have anything like the same impact as in the days of the unreformed Roman rite. Dramatic reading of the passion gospel can heighten the first part of the service on this day.

Next comes the Proclamation of the Cross. Once again, the Roman liturgy is adapted, both by the title of this part of the liturgy as well as in the explanatory notes, which stress the need to vary the way in which this section of the service is prepared and presented. In fact, variation was clearly the order of the day when the veneration of the cross spread to the West. In one Roman rite, which dates from the end of the eighth century, the bishop leads the introit procession, swinging a censer (a very Eastern-looking practice - what Western bishop in his right senses would ever perform such a menial task?). The pontifical thurifer censes the cross while the procession moves up the church, and the liturgy begins with the veneration, after which the Word-service is celebrated. A later rite adopts the (to us familiar) order, and venerates the cross *after* the Word.

Earlier rites place the cross on the altar. Later rites place it conveniently nearer the congregation. Mediterranean temperament finds kissing the cross natural, as do many North Europeans today. But there is nothing gained in laying down the law about how the veneration is performed. Late medieval rites elaborated on the approach to the cross, with three genuflexions, each accompanied by a long devotional prayer. The antiphon, *Ecce lignum crucis* ('Behold the wood of the cross') has a long-standing tradition, but it probably refers to the 'wood' of an alleged relic of the true cross. This kind of thing is clearly secondary, like the method of venerating.

The new service provides for no fewer than four anthems during the 'veneration', though other hymns and devotions may be used. The *first* ('We glory in your cross') adapts the first anthem in the Roman rite at this point, which first appears in the ninth century Senlis Antiphonal mentioned earlier, but is probably of Greek origin. The *second* is a new composition, specially composed (among other things) to avoid anti-Semitism; its style is comparable to the traditional 'Reproaches', the text of which is not included, though the rubric would permit its use. Many will lament the omission, on grounds of suspected anti-Semitism, of this old hymn, inspired by biblical reflection and earlier Jerusalem usage. It is to be found in both JLG and the Roman rite. The *third* ('You are worthy . . .': Rev. 4.11; 5.9, 10, 13b) is taken from the Friday evening canticle in the JLG *Daily Office* (1968). It stresses the paschal character of Good Friday in a proclamatory way, whereas the new Reproaches take a more penitential attitude. Finally, the fourth anthem ('We adore you, O Christ') comes from David Silk's *Prayers for Use at the Alternative Services*; the main part is from 1 Tim. 3.16. Thus the chants at the 'Proclamation' are a mixture of various traditions. But local hymns and songs may be equally appropriate.

The Intercession in the old Roman rite was made up of biddings and collects, interspersed with silences, during which the faithful knelt down. These biddings and collects probably go right back to the third (in the case of the biddings) and fourth (in the case of the collects) centuries, and they offer the most important paradigm for intercessory prayer which the Western churches possess in their repertoire. Many congregations in the Anglican tradition are accustomed to this format at the conclusion of the offices of Mattins and Evensong. A bidding normally pinpoints a specific subject of prayer and it is usually extempore. Then a suitable collect, from one of the several anthologies available, sums up the topic in a general manner. Thus bidding is specific, collect is universal.

Since in many congregations there have been experiments in wide forms of participation in intercession during the Sunday Eucharist, it is vital that the Good Friday liturgy avoids their more banal manifestations, especially as on this day the Church contemplates a sacrifice, and true intercession is sacrificial in its character. Whereas the Roman Missal (1970) reforms the old texts and themes, new adaptations (JLG and American Prayer Book) tend to simplify. The new service has five themes for prayer: the Church; the Nations; the Jews; Unbelievers; and the Suffering. Each is abundantly appropriate for the day. The biddings follow the American Prayer Book and adapt them. They come across clearly as items addressed *to the congregation*. The collects are addressed *to God*; and they come from various sources. The first is a modern version of the second collect for Good Friday in the Prayer Book (1662). The second comes from the 1968 Remembrance Sunday Service, as this appears in David Silk's collection. The third, for the Jews, is the work of the Liturgical Commission; it tries to avoid anti-Semitism, as well as pray for the mission of the Church in such a way as not to patronize Judaism. The fourth and fifth both adapt texts from the American Prayer Book.

The new service also permits the Litany as a form of solemn intercession. It is important to follow a special form on this day so that the character of the liturgy makes its own impression on the congregation. (The compilers of the first Prayer Books were sufficiently impressed by the old 'Solemn Prayers' to prepare three - not one - collects for Good Friday.)

82

Communion?

Finally, the question of communion raises itself. Following Anglican adaptations, significantly the American Prayer Book (1979), provision is made for three options; no communion, communion from the reserved sacrament, or a full celebration of the Eucharist. No special explanation of the first and the third of these options is necessary; the first is undoubtedly the most ancient (and the most common among non-Roman Catholic Christians today); the third has some Reformation precedent. The second appears at Rome in the seventh and eighth centuries, but the directions in these forms suggest that it was not universally popular, even though reservation was made in both kinds. From the ninth century, only the consecrated host was reserved, and there was a decline in the number of communicants in many places, though in some religious establishments, general communion persisted (several of the seventeenth- and eighteenth-century 'Neo-Gallican' liturgies of France also had a general communion). In the later Middle Ages, as we observed in the previous chapter, the procession to and from the place of the 'repose' became more and more elaborate, so that the Reformers (most of whom did not approve of the reserved sacrament anyway) decided that this was an aspect of liturgical tradition that could go. However, many Anglicans are accustomed to receiving communion in this way, and for them, the 'Mass of the presanctified' (since Vatican II a general communion – no longer just the priest) is an appropriate way of avoiding the presumption of a Eucharist while at the same time expressing the need for communion and the dependence upon God's grace.

The liturgical books of the 'Gelasian' tradition, which date from the eighth century, clearly want to link communion and veneration, in order to provide a rationale for this method of receiving communion. Accordingly, the veneration and communion happen at the same time. On the other hand, the older French ('Gallican') and Spanish ('Visigothic') traditions happily did without this communion. History, therefore, provides no clear 'answer', and local congregations will no doubt come to their own conclusions about what is the best and most appropriate way. But whichever of the options is adopted, the new services provide an austere ending to the liturgy, with the ASB collect for Lent 5 as an evocative liturgical full-stop.

Using the 1986 Service

There is no day in the liturgical year when the pattern of worship needs more careful review in most churches than Good Friday. Through a series of developments, Anglicans have, more often than not, found themselves with a barren sort of service, with little liturgical shape, Scripture only in snippets, and far too much reliance on the persuasiveness of a preacher. The liturgical material of the day, including the St John passion, has been within the service of 'Ante Communion', sometimes preceded by Mattins and Litany, but this has been celebrated at an early hour with only a handful of people present, while most church-goers have come to a Family Service mid-morning, a three hour preaching service (or part of it), from 12 to 3, or an ecumenical act of witness. All these have their value, but there is a real loss when the liturgical material available for the day is not incorporated within them, and especially when the great biblical passages of the day (notably Isaiah 52—53 and the Johannine account of the passion) are not read in their entirety. The pattern of the day needs rethinking to give them the prominence they deserve.

In many places the right time to celebrate the main service will be at 1.30 or 2 o'clock so that it may reach its conclusion around the time of our Lord's death. A 2 o'clock 'Hour at the Cross' is well established in many places and the form provided in *Lent, Holy Week, Easter* is very suitable for use at such an hour. Where there is a 'three hour' tradition, this needs to be taken seriously and not undermined. But it is very possible to retain the first part of it as the time-honoured preaching service and to use it as a preparation for the liturgy that will begin at 1.30 or 2. Where this is done, it will be important, however, for people to realize that the three hours have become a developing service that builds to a climax, and that it will be better for those who do not come for the whole three hours to come during it and stay, than to come at the beginning and go!

But there is, of course, a new difficulty about the timing of Good Friday services that arises from the increasing practice of shop and factory opening throughout this day. For many it is no longer a day off work. Sad as it may be, for the early afternoon is the natural time for the liturgy on Good Friday, a new pattern may have to be adopted in many places whereby the service is celebrated in early evening. If at all possible, it should be in daylight.

A word may be said about vesture on Good Friday. There has developed a rather eccentric Anglican tradition of dispensing with alb or surplice on Good Friday, and for clergy, servers and choir to wear only the cassock. Although this does no harm, and a distinctiveness of dress may add to the special feel of the day, it can reinforce that false picture of Good Friday as a kind of 'day of mourning' for our Lord. It is not that, but a sensitive celebration of the power of the cross. The white of alb or surplice is quite appropriate, as is the liturgical colour of red, for the martyr King by whose blood we are redeemed, in the vestments of the clergy.

The introductory notes to the Good Friday service lay very special emphasis on the place of silence in today's liturgy. It is both an identification with Christ in his silent suffering and also the natural response to the story of our salvation. The liturgy begins and ends in silence (no organ music, no bells, no idle chatter) and the high points within it - the passion reading, the proclamation of the cross, the sharing in the consecrated elements - elicit a response of silence. The service therefore begins, as it will continue, by a silent entry of the ministers (section 1) who go to their places and kneel for a while in silent prayer (section 2), after which the president alone stands to say the collect (section 3).

The Ministry of the Word that now follows is not, on this occasion, to be shortened by the omission of any of the readings, though the use at section 6 of the long option of Hebrews 10.1-25 would seem inappropriate in most settings after the long Isaiah passage. Psalm 22.1-22, whether said or sung, is clearly an important part of the scripture recitation for today. Since there has been no hymn at the beginning of the service, a hymn is the most likely choice at section 7 before the passion gospel. Questions relating to the reading of the passion have already been discussed as they apply to Palm Sunday (see page 52). Where the people have all joined in the 'crowd' scenes on Palm Sunday, there is a strong case for their listening *silently* today, with only a small group as a representative 'crowd', and, whereas on Palm Sunday, after all the standing of the procession, an argument can be made for sitting for part of the passion reading, on Good Friday, where there is much sitting and kneeling, there is a strong case for standing *throughout* the passion reading. The reading over, there is need for a short response of silence, still standing, before the sermon.

Although a rubric provides that the Proclamation of the Cross may be held over until after the Intercession (as in the Roman rite), *Lent, Holy Week, Easter* does urge that it follow now, adding a visual dimension to what the Ministry of the Word has proclaimed, and providing, in the wooden cross, a focus for the Intercession offered 'at the foot of the cross'. The rubrics also provide for the omission of this whole stage (sections 12-17) of the service, but that would be a grave impoverishment. At its most simple, the Proclamation of the Cross is the setting up or displaying of a plain wooden cross and prayers, silent and spoken, with the cross as the focus. It may be enhanced by music, both hymns and anthems, and may include movement, both of the cross and of the people, but these are not absolutely necessary. At least in its most simple form, it deserves a place in this liturgy wherever it is celebrated.

Where a wooden cross has been part of the Good Friday service in the past, it has sometimes been in the sanctuary veiled from the beginning of the service and is, at this point, unveiled. This remains a possibility, but far better that the minister go to the back of the church, returning with one carrying it on high slowly through the church to the prominent position where it is to be placed. The minister is not imitating Christ: he does not drag the cross on his shoulder. He carries it aloft as the sign of victory. Nevertheless he should carry it himself, rather than delegate it to servers. The prominent position to which it is carried, and where it will normally need to be placed in a firm base, may be the chancel step, the altar top, or the east wall, depending on local circumstances.

It may be borne through the church in silence (and, where there is no choir, this would be best, for the people do not want to be so deep in their hymn books that they fail to see this slow movement through the church), or the great hymn of the passion, 'Sing, my tongue, the glorious battle . . . Faithful cross, above all other, one and only noble tree', may be sung. The main hymn books include it, though some translations are better than others. There is an attractive verse that most versions do not include early in the hymn:

> Hear the helpless baby crying
> Where the narrow manger stands
> See how she, his Virgin Mother,
> Ties his limbs with slender bands,
> Swaddling clothes she wraps about him,
> And confines God's feet and hands.

How many verses of this long hymn are to be used will depend a great deal on the size of the church and length of the procession. It can be very effective to set out the hymn so that verses alternate between choir and 'all'. During the verses that all sing the procession stands still; during the choir verses, it advances a little further through the church.

The cross is then placed in its prominent place and all kneel. The anthems provided may be sung or said, or other material may be substituted. The anthems are set out with parts for leader and people, and so may be spoken responsively, where singing of them would be too difficult. In most circumstances it would be unnecessary, and would destroy the balance of the service, to use them all. But both Anthem 3 (section 16) and 4 (section 17) would make suitable doxologies to the use of the new Reproaches.

A word must be said here about the omission of the text of the traditional Reproaches. These had been included in the first published version and are to be included in *Prayers for use at the Alternative Services* (2nd Edition 1986). The omission of this anthem, and its replacement by a new version, is a response to the suspicion of anti-Semitism. Although it is clear that anti-Semitism has never been intended, in these sensitive days it has sometimes been perceived, and this must certainly be borne in mind in making a selection of anthems. Nevertheless, many will be grateful that the Liturgical Commission has at least permitted the use of the traditional Reproaches by a rubric that speaks of other 'suitable hymns and anthems'. Because the Reproaches capture the mood of Good Friday in a way that none of the alternatives are quite able to achieve, they are indeed suitable and highly appropriate.

The 'appropriate devotions' to which the rubric (section 13) refers may in some churches include the movement of the people forward to the cross one by one, there to kneel for a moment in prayer or to kiss it. Others will deprecate this more individual devotion, and much prefer a corporate response of prayer by the whole congregation without any movement from where each kneels. But, again, it is clear that the heart of the response to the proclamation of the cross is the silence that is ordered after the anthem.

This section of the service may end with a hymn (section 18). Where the anthems have been sung, this will be somewhat superfluous. But where they have been spoken, a musical ending to the devotion will be right. Isaac Watts' 'When I survey' has a special claim at this point, with the congregation still kneeling.

The Intercession (sections 19 and 20) follows the ancient pattern of the solemn prayers on this day. The biddings could well be read by lay people, but the collects are, at least on this occasion, best said by the president, as he stands at the foot of the cross. The form provided has a solemnity about it that suits the day and it will not be improved by extempore interpolation. The ASB Litany, which is a permitted alternative, has the same gravity about it, but the invitation to use 'other suitable words' will be best resisted; it would be difficult to improve on what is provided. After a long period of kneeling for the 'Proclamation of the Cross', standing might be the best posture for intercession on this day.

Careful consideration will need to be given to the question of whether to bring the service to its conclusion with the sharing of Holy Communion. For the majority of Anglicans this will be novel and, if it is to be done, will need careful preparation. *Lent, Holy Week, Easter,* while acknowledging the validity of the position of those who prefer to abstain from communion from Maundy Thursday until Easter, nevertheless comes down quite heavily in favour of including the sacramental sharing. Early practice and liturgical history is more sympathetic to the abstinence view and might cause some to hesitate before abandoning their previous practice. If there is to be no Holy Communion, the service is best brought to an end with a hymn, after the Intercession, and then the Lord's Prayer (section 33) and single collect (section 34). The omission of blessing and dismissal and the departure in silence are important.

But if Holy Communion is to be the final stage of the service, as the mainstream text encourages, a decision has to be made as to whether there is to be a *celebration* or reception from the elements set aside on Maundy Thursday night. The latter presupposes a view of Maundy Thursday and Good Friday that sees them as a continuum, with the watch drawing together the two liturgies between which it is placed. It also presupposes a theology of reservation or 'extended distribution' that not all would easily accept. There does seem to be a certain oddity about receiving the consecrated bread and wine twice from the same celebration. On the other hand, if one believes that a full celebration detracts from the sacrifice of Calvary that this day proclaims, but that sharing in the consecrated elements is an important way of entering fully and sacramentally into his experience - proclaiming his death until he comes again - the use of presanctified bread and wine may be the best option.

If there is to be a celebration, it begins with the Preparation of the Gifts. A hymn may be sung while this is done. The emphasis is on simplicity. A procession with the elements would be wrong, 'offertory' sentences or prayers out of place. In silence the president places a white cloth on the bare altar and then sufficient bread and wine. He 'takes' them into his hands and then begins the Eucharistic Prayer. A note suggests the particular suitability of the Fourth Eucharistic Prayer, with its passion-penitence emphasis, with either preface 9 or 10. Thereafter Rite A is followed normally until all have received Holy Communion, though it would be wholly appropriate to break the bread in silence and to introduce the Invitation, 'Jesus is the Lamb of God . . .' (section 28) before the Distribution. Music should be used sparingly, and silence might be better then hymnody during the Distribution.

Where the presanctified elements are to be used for the Distribution, the procedure is more simple. Once the cloth has been laid on the table, the consecrated bread and wine are brought to the altar. There is nothing to encourage communion only in one kind today, and it should not have been difficult to keep consecrated wine in a flagon. The wine is now poured into a chalice. The Lord's Prayer (section 25) is said and the *Agnus Dei* (section 26) is permitted, though it is superfluous, since it is an anthem to cover the Breaking of the Bread (which will not happen if this is not a full celebration). The Invitation includes the material from the ASB Rite A appendix, 'Jesus is the Lamb of God . . .', so that, even where the *Agnus Dei* has not been said, the Lamb of God theology does receive expression. If there is to be a further hymn after the Distribution, it will need to follow the silence and precede the concluding collect with which the service abruptly ends. If it is three o'clock or later, a hymn that introduces the element of the Lord's burial may seem right. Selected verses from Archbishop Maclagan's 'It is finished! blessed Jesus' would be suitable. But there is a strong argument for no music at all after communion.

Lent, Holy Week, Easter says nothing about *children* on Good Friday. This is a day on which there is very frequently a well-established service involving children. Their needs must be taken seriously and met. Yet it is difficult to see how the younger of these could take part fully in the liturgy as described, with its strong emphasis on stillness and silence. Of course this is only the same challenge that parishes face every Sunday, but it is 'writ large' on Good Friday. Without departing from the basic principle that families should worship together, at least for part of the liturgy, each Sunday, perhaps it can be argued that Good Friday *is* different, for children cannot enter into the meaning of Christ's passion in the same way as adults, though they can respond in their own way to the story of Holy Week. It is probably best that on this day the children should worship at their own level at a different time or place. It may be earlier in the morning; it may be at the same time as the liturgy but in the church hall (and this latter is more likely to set their parents free to be in church). But, whenever and wherever they do meet, it is a very simplified *liturgy* that will best meet their need too. They need to hear the story read or see it acted. They need a cross as the focus for worship. They can be helped so to enter into it all that they too can be silent for a short while at the foot of the cross. Recognizing that their needs are slightly different, and their level of understanding less sophisticated, need not involve us in underestimating their response to the story that the Good Friday liturgy proclaims.

91

Easter

'Every Eucharist is Easter Day'

Is there not a Passover of the Church every Sunday? Surely some new victim is not offered in that feast? Surely the Passover is not one immolation, and the Eucharist another? Surely there is not one beautiful mystery in the Passover, and then another one on Sunday, and Wednesday and Friday? For as often as you make the memorial of the passion of Christ, you make Passover.

We have seen many examples so far of the way in which the 'historical' attitude of the fourth century left its mark on Christian worship. The earlier 'unitive' spirituality which celebrated the death and resurrection all at once, and overnight, was replaced by a piety which brought the most important 'events' leading up to Christ's burial and resurrection into special prominence. Hence what Egeria witnessed at Jerusalem, where special ceremonies sharpen the religious focus through such customs as the palm procession, the veneration of the cross, and the ambiance of being in Jerusalem and celebrating these things. The next stage was the liturgical trade-route, as effective in antiquity as it is today.

The passage quoted above is a sort of rhetorical rearguard action. It comes from one of the homilies of Severian of Gabala, who flourished towards the end of the fourth century. His cautionary words insist that the Passover is not to supersede the Eucharist, since the Eucharist, in order to have a reality of its own, is a Passover, a celebration of the death and resurrection of Christ. There is something marvellously wholesome about the spirituality of this short passage, and the allusion to Paul's command to repeat (1 Cor. 11.26) would not be missed by many of his hearers. The Passover as an annual celebration is not to overshadow the Eucharist, celebrated on the first day of the week, the day of the resurrection, nor should it overshadow celebrations on the two Christian fast-days, Wednesday and Friday.

Such an insistence on every Sunday as Easter Day recurs in history. Nearer home, it occurs in the Danish Lutheran tradition among its greatest hymnwriters, Thomas Kingo (a seventeenth-century Bishop of Odense), Hans Brorson (an eighteenth-century Bishop of Ribe) and Nikolai Grundtvig (the nineteenth-century Danish equivalent of England's John Wesley). Among Grundtvig's compositions which are most popular in Denmark today ranks one hymn which contains the following verses, full of Easter allusions, including liturgical ones (Grundtvig was an adept translator of old Latin and Greek hymnology). Appropriately, the hymn starts, 'Built on the Rock the church doth stand', and stanzas 3, 5, and 6 go thus:

> We are God's house of living stones,
> builded for his habitation;
> He through baptismal grace us owns,
> Heirs of his wondrous salvation;
> Were we but two his name to tell,
> Yet, he would deign with us to dwell,
> With all his grace and his favour.

> Here stands the font before our eyes,
> Telling how God did receive us;
> Th'altar recalls Christ's sacrifice
> And what his table doth give us;
> Here sounds the Word that doth proclaim
> Christ yesterday, today the same,
> Yea, and for aye our Redeemer.

> Grant then, O God, where'er men roam,
> That when the church bells are ringing,
> Many in Jesus' faith may come
> Where he his message is bringing:
> I know mine own, mine own know me,
> Ye, not the world, my face shall see:
> My peace I leave with you. Amen.

(The translation misses several of the biblical/liturgical allusions,

including the last line of stanza 6, which quotes the Danish
Lutheran formula at the Peace in the Eucharist.)

Easter, then, is not to be confined. But it gains in impact in
two ways. At its best, Easter can build up a healthy spirituality
all the year round when it is itself celebrated in an authentic
manner. The fact that the renewal of liturgy in this century
began with Easter is no coincidence, and it would be a pity if
there were Anglican congregations which, for the rest of the
year, were happy to introduce special liturgical practices but
somehow denied the possibilities inherent in Easter. Of course
there are obstacles. One is the folk piety which still insists that
Easter is a day which is best celebrated by a straight morning
Eucharist; and folk piety, especially when emphasized by
crowds of annual (or bi-annual) communicants, is a difficult
phenomenon to confront and change. As we have observed
already, liturgy (which includes folk piety) is resistant to change
on special occasions.

Symbolism

So far, we have discussed the history of liturgy a great deal. But
history for its own sake is not enough, nor, indeed, should the
faithful feel debarred from entering into the spirit of these old
liturgies in their modern form before they have passed some
history examination. It is, however, important, that the history is
easily available to those who plan worship in local congregations,
and also for those who want to read more. But symbolism in
liturgy should not have to be explained in order to carry many
levels of meaning. Indeed, in some respects, the more that it *is*
explained, the *fewer* the levels of meaning that can be engaged
through the senses and perceptions of individual worshippers at
the celebration itself. This is not an argument against *all* forms
of explanation in the liturgy; but it is a caution against lengthy,
ill-prepared and unimaginative ones.

Two of the criticisms most commonly hurled at the new
liturgies (in all the Western churches that have undergone
schemes for revision) is that they are (say some) ephemeral and
follow trendy ways, and (say others) they are so ancient that

they have nothing to say to our century. 'We have aimed to preserve a proper continuity with the past, but with freshness', writes the Chairman of the Commission, Douglas Jones, perhaps to counter both these criticisms. Undoubtedly, the best advertisement for the new services is a congregation that takes them into its own heart, and celebrates them prayerfully and thoughtfully. And if there is a tension at Easter between the 'regulars' and those who come along expecting things as they were fifty years ago, this is only a recurrence of a problem churches have long had to deal with. For example, in a traditional, medieval Lincolnshire parish church, the Easter Vigil (inspired by the 1930 *Directory*'s shortened form) was attended by only a small number, and there was no possibility of bringing the crowds who attended the main Easter Eucharist and Easter Evensong to a late night liturgy the day before, or (for that matter) a very early Eucharist. Accordingly, the Easter morning Sung Eucharist began at the font (at the back of the church), with the lighting of the paschal candle, while the introductory part of the *Exultet* was sung, alternating between deacon and choirmen. The paschal candle then led the procession up the nave of the church, making an impressive change from the customary processional cross. The Eucharist, printed in full, ended with the traditional acclamation - 'The Lord is risen - He is risen indeed - ALLELUIA!' Then at the end of Evensong, there was a procession to the font, and the whole congregation renewed its baptismal vows, with prayers and hymns to interpret this solemn, annual rite.

Clearly, there are many churches which could be much more adventurous, and it is for these that the Easter Liturgy has been composed. In some respects, this service is the most well thought out in the entire anthology, which is all the better, because the Easter Liturgy, with its Vigil and its Service of Light, runs counter to so many Easter traditions in this country. But before we enter its details, it is important to say something about the world in which it operates and moves - the world of symbolism.

Symbols are not the same as signs, and yet many liturgical presidents (and faithful, too) prefer to turn symbols into signs, so that everything is predefined, neat, and tidy. The differences lie in such observations as these. Signs are performative, and reach a predetermined end: symbols express an intention, and achieve their end at the same time. Signs manipulate; symbols do not, because they resound and suggest. Signs do not express but perform; symbols do not perform, but achieve what they signify. Signs do not communicate at the personal level; symbols communicate creatively at the personal level, and are part of a real 'encounter'. All this means that the symbols of Holy Week are not taken in at a glance, because they are meant to help us to continue to relate to things, truths, realities which a signpost cannot convey. The driver of a car would not know what to do if faced with a road sign which had a cross on it; nor, by contrast, would the faithful on Palm Sunday if suddenly given a 'No Entry' sign instead of a palm cross, and if she/he were given that sign, it would doubtless be taken to suggest something else . . . perhaps a 'deeper meaning' . . . Symbols, especially when new, engender some degree of self-consciousness, and this is why the first time special liturgies which (it is hoped) will be repeated annually are introduced, it is of the utmost importance that details are thought about by those who plan them, so that the second time round there is some sense of rhythm. For without rhythm - even on special occasions that are relatively new - ordinary worshippers are unlikely to engage with the liturgy at any deep level, and the new rites will have already lost their potential in lasting value because they have degenerated into being just one more service. Above all, the Easter Liturgy is a sacrament of *encounter* between the risen Christ and the faithful, so that the non-verbal symbolisms that are used should be as lavish as the verbal. Easter hymns which congregations enjoy singing so much are full of judicious repetition; and an Easter sermon, however carefully constructed, is likely to have a single theme which unfolds in various guises. Therefore, whether you are dealing with candles, water, oil, perfume, or walking from one point to another, there is little to be gained, and probably everything to be lost, by interpreting liturgical directions (or suggestions) in a *clinical* and *minimalistic* manner. The Easter Liturgy is not the occasion for domesticating some of the most ancient customs of Christianity into a neat, Anglo-Saxon milieu, where everything has its proper place, and the liturgy feels like a computer print-out.

The Easter Liturgy - Shape

The Easter Liturgy in the new services is derived from four basic ingredients, which probably go back to at least the third century. The first is the fact that the liturgy is a vigil, and therefore needs some light: hence light that is both functional and symbolic. The second is the ingredient needful to a vigil: a series of biblical readings, with chants and prayers between them, for reflection and natural pause. The third is the baptismal liturgy, the climax of the long time of preparation for the lucky catechumens of that year. And the fourth is the Easter Eucharist, which only comes as a result of that internal logic, that watching and waiting. And the traditional time for both the baptism and the Eucharist was dawn, which, in the Mediterranean world in late spring is earlier than in the North of Europe.

Easter is a sacrament of encounter. But an encounter presupposes two (or more) persons. In the first centuries, the word 'Pascha' ('Passover': Latin, *passio*) was first of all interpreted as 'passion': 'Christ our Passover is sacrificed for us' (1 Cor. 5.6). In this understanding, Christ is the protagonist. During the third century (when baptisms came to be restricted to Easter), another interpretation gained popularity, of 'Pascha' as 'passing': 'Before the feast of Passover Jesus, knowing that his hour had come to pass from this world to the Father . . .' (John 13.1). In this understanding, however, it is not Jesus who is the protagonist, it is the *Christian*. The result of these two (complementary) interpretations is that there are two, historic views of Holy Week that have coexisted for centuries. On the one hand, Holy Week is a series of 'events' which are celebrated. On the other hand, Holy Week is a 'mystery in which the Christian grows'. It is the latter view which dominates the Easter Liturgy, largely because it was most popular at the time when the Easter Liturgy was undergoing its basic development.

Unfortunately, Egeria has little to say about the character of the Easter Liturgy (or Vigil, as it is usually called) at Jerusalem, because it resembled what she knew from home. But she notes special treatment of the baptism candidates, for they are led straight from the font to the Anastasis (Church of the Resurrection), where the bishop says a special prayer for them. However, we can reconstruct that liturgy as consisting of all four features, light, vigil lections, baptism, and Eucharist. The question-marks hover only around the nature of the light ceremonies. Probably, they amounted to a special version of the lamp-lighting which Egeria notes as a regular feature of vespers. There is little difference between the ceremonial lighting of lamps at vespers and the special Easter ceremonies of light which grew up in the Eastern churches, since they share a basic similarity, in that they all understand these lights as an 'epiphany' of Christ, the light of the world. To this day, the Byzantine rite churches begin vespers with a solemn lighting of candles while the hymn *phos hilaron* is sung. They also recreate the later Jerusalem practice of lighting candles and processing with them, before Easter Mattins and Eucharist; but there is no special blessing over one 'paschal' candle; rather, there is a prayer over the candles after their distribution, which dwells on the theme of light, and asks for the presence of Christ as the illuminator of the hearts and minds of the Christian community.

By contrast, the Western churches fastened on to the notion of *one* special 'paschal' candle, to stand in pre-eminence over all others, and this probably gave rise to the practice of a solemn blessing, given by the deacon; this is what has later come to be called the *Exultet*, from the opening word of its first strophe, 'Rejoice, heavenly powers'. It is conceivable that such a solemn blessing, after the sharing of the light among the faithful, arose in the north of Italy, which may partially explain the later insertion of passages from Vergil's *Georgics IV*. (Vergil came from Mantua.) Several different versions appear in local service-books, where it is frequently called the *laus cerei* ('praise of the candle'), a title which clearly shows the difference between the Eastern and Western mentalities in this regard. At first, the prayer began with the eucharistic dialogue, but the introductory

Exultet was added, which first appears in the 'Gothic Missal' (written at the beginning of the eighth century in Luxeuil, reflecting old French traditions, rather than Roman). The threefold structure of introduction, dialogue, and preface became standard in the West. The chant was originally that of the Canon of the Mass, but soon the *Exultet* developed its own elaborate music, to interpret its very special characteristics on a solemn day of the year. Two important versions of the chant were in circulation in the Middle Ages, Beneventan and Norman, but the latter eventually replaced the former in the thirteenth century when the Norman invasion reached the centre of Italy.

When the new services were being compiled, the Commission had to look with great care at the shape of this Liturgy, because two divergent structures were in circulation in this country. On the one hand, the Roman Missal (1970) reproduced the traditional order, of light, vigil lections, eucharistic synaxis, baptism, and eucharistic liturgy from the offertory onwards. On the other hand, the JLG order (both 1971 and 1983) *inverted* the order, so that the vigil lections and eucharistic synaxis took place in semi-darkness, to be followed by the ceremonies of light, and then baptism and Eucharist. The advantage of the Roman order is that it is traditional. The advantage of the JLG structure is that it makes the Vigil into a real Vigil, so that the darkness builds up a sense of waiting and watching.

The Easter Liturgy as we have it appears to opt for a typically Anglican compromise! In fact, the Commission looked carefully at the history of this ancient liturgy in the East after Egeria, and found a crucial adaptation of history in the tenth-century liturgy of the Jerusalem monastery of the Holy Cross, which probably reflects earlier Jerusalem practice. In this document the Easter Liturgy comprised the following basic items:

vespers of the burial of Christ
phos hilaron (= 'Hail, gladdening light', vesper-light hymn)
vigil readings
The Light: shared from the tomb

end of vespers
baptisms
Eucharist: synaxis and sacrament.

There is much that is complex in the history of this scheme, but it is not appropriate to discuss it here. Suffice it to say that the main rationale for the service is to distinguish between a basic, functional vesper-light, for the vigil readings (on the one hand), and the symbolic Easter light, shared by all, in a blaze of glory (on the other hand). This blaze is all the more dramatic in coming from Christ's tomb. And this rationale is explained also by the different contexts in which different units of Scripture are read. For the *vigil* lections are read in semi-darkness, because they represent the waiting and watching Church, poring over the Old Testament, whereas the *eucharistic synaxis*-lections proclaim the Easter gospel, and therefore are accompanied by the symbolism of light. It is, perhaps, a mark of the impoverishment of modern liturgies that we cannot read Scripture in more than one liturgical context, and this weakness is reflected in both the Roman (1970) and the JLG (1971 and 1983) structures, where vigil lections lead straight into eucharistic synaxis. But, in line with permitted variations of shape elsewhere in these services, the traditional Roman structure may be followed.

The Easter Liturgy - Content

The new service begins with an introduction, based on the new Roman. For the vigil lections, there is ample provision of Old Testament readings, with psalms and collects to match them. There are no fewer than 12 lections, many of which occur in other modern rites; 1, 3, 4, 5, 7, 8, 10 and 12 occur in the new Roman rite; 2 (the fall) appears in the old Spanish rite; 6 (entry to the promised land) is a traditional reading, often found in the medieval lectionaries; 11 is also traditional, and occurs in the American Episcopal Prayer Book (1979); 9 (the fear of mortality, Job 14.1-14) does not appear in any known Easter Liturgy, but it appears in the ASB as the Old Testament reading for the Saturday after Easter. While the psalms connect well with the lections, the collects (all from ASB) are dull by comparison.

The Service of Light consists of the three stages which are traditional in the West, though there is scope for considerable adaptation. First, the Easter candle (as it is called) is lit. Secondly, the candle is carried through the church. Thirdly, the candle is placed on its stand, and solemnly blessed, with a form of the new Roman Catholic *Exultet*. At the first stage, a short prayer for illumination (from the American Prayer Book of 1979) leads into three short formulae (all Roman Catholic, 1970) which can accompany the signing of the candle, the insertion of the 'incense grains', and the lighting of the candle. (Many people omit the 'incense grains', which are a late medieval accretion, based on a misunderstanding of an old formula for blessing the paschal candle with a (smaller) lighted candle.) Another custom is to mark the number of the calendar year on the candle, with Heb. 13.8 providing a suitable formula. The second stage has the most dramatic possibilities, which the old Spanish rite exploited to the full, imitating previous Jerusalem practice, with a sudden blaze of light emerging from behind a sacristy door. In the Middle Ages, two customs interpreted the 'entry' of the light. One was to sing a hymn. The other was to halt at certain points and shout *'Lumen Christi'*. The latter gained eventual acceptance at Rome, and it is the one used in the new service. Finally, the third stage consists of the *Exultet*. The text given is an adaptation of the JLG and new Roman (1970) versions. Certain themes are left out from the latter, including the (now optional) 'happy fault' strophe, which was deliberately omitted from several local books in the Middle Ages, including the Cluniac version (Hugh did not approve) and the Romano-Germanic Pontifical; the Germans and Danes followed suit, though not the Swedes! The new version reads well, and restores the traditional threefold 'This is the night' which JLG lost. The Passover theology of the *Exultet* repays careful study. Moreover, the new suggested order places the gospel immediately before the *Exultet*, unless it is read later. Such a juxtaposition reflects the preferred understanding of the function of light in this Liturgy that we have already noted.

At the eucharistic synaxis, the collect is that of ASB (adapted from 1928), the epistle is Roman (1970) and JLG, and the gospel is one of three (Roman, 1970). Interestingly enough, the epistle pericope ('dying and rising with Christ', Rom. 6.3-11) was traditional at this Liturgy only in France, in the old Gallican rite. This takes us to the Liturgy of Initiation. The introductory notes recommend strongly that there should be a baptism and/or confirmation at this service, and there will be many congregations in which this is already popular. Such a restoration is far more significant than the renewal of baptismal vows, which (as we have noted already) was introduced only when the Vigil was restored in 1951 in the Roman Catholic Church and which many find somewhat artificial. (The text for the renewal is taken from ASB with an alternative extended text in an appendix.) In the Eucharist, the traditional acclamation may be used at the Peace. The Post-Communion Prayer is one of the most beautiful in use today; it is an old Spanish prayer, and appears in the version contained in David Silk's collection, *Prayers for Use at the Alternative Services.*

The new Easter Liturgy incorporates and adapts tradition. Its shape has been carefully worked out on the basis of an examination of the evidence as well as what it is thought will 'work' in local congregations. Clearly the Liturgy of Easter night will be at its most effective when it is long, and feels like hard work. One of the problems with it during the Middle Ages (and after) was that its anticipation on Saturday morning meant that it became a mere relic rather than the vibrant heart of the Easter community. An additional provision in the vigil lections for this service is the synoptic passion narratives. Such an option certainly underlines the 'passover-as-passing' view of the Easter Liturgy, wherein the Christian passes from death to life, an experience which a lengthy and carefully thought out liturgy may do a great deal to bring forth in ordinary congregations. On the other hand, the service may be phased through the night, and end at dawn; the options are many. The important sequel to all this, however, is that the Easter festival should lead into a *season*, and that Easter is not confined to a spring morning, as

Severian of Gabala and Nikolai Grundtvig (in their different ways) have already pungently reminded us.

Using the 1986 Service

The introductory notes to this service lay particular emphasis on the unity of the rite, how both baptism (or at least the renewal of vows) and Eucharist are the proper and natural climax of the Easter Liturgy. This emphasis is intended to counter a tendency to separate the Vigil and the Service of Light from the material that follows, using the first on Saturday evening and the remainder on Sunday morning. The whole tone of this section of *Lent, Holy Week, Easter* is against such a division. It deprecates also a cut-off point after the baptismal material with the plea that 'the natural and proper climax of the whole Easter Liturgy is the Eucharist, in which we are sacramentally reunited with our risen Lord. This should not be omitted from the celebration except for serious reason', though it does provide an ending for a liturgy without Holy Communion. The only division of material that it does countenance, where there is need, is to make a separate service of the 'Vigil', by which it means the time of readings, psalmody, collects and silence. But, when this happens, the Service of Light should be attached to the Easter morning liturgy of baptism and Eucharist. Once the paschal candle has been lit and the Easter proclamation made, it is odd and unsatisfying to put on the brakes until all has been achieved in the sharing of Easter communion.

Questions about the unity or division of the rite are obviously related to the matter of time. *Lent, Holy Week, Easter* lays emphasis on the dawn as the very best time for the liturgy to reach the stages of baptism and Eucharist. But it is also clear that the ideal is to start in darkness, for both the vigil and the Service of Light are most effective in darkness. This would point to a service beginning at some time during the hours of darkness and ending a little after dawn. There *are* parishes where it happens, and every encouragement should be given to others where it could 'catch on' to try it this way, but it would be very

103

unfortunate if clergy and parishes that knew such a timing was not for them, dismissed this whole service from their thinking.

A celebration entirely during the hours of darkness is by no means a poor second best. After all, it is only the *discovery* of the empty tomb that the Scriptures attribute to Easter morning and even that 'very early in the morning while it was still dark'. The resurrection event, that no one witnessed, belongs to the night, and a celebration of a great victory of light over darkness is appropriately expressed where darkness is driven out by a flood of candle light. Of course, when it is entirely a night celebration, the Eucharist has a different feel about it, and those who communicate at it will probably feel the need to return on Sunday morning to share in a different sort of celebration, where the emphasis seems to be much less on the victory of light over darkness, and much more on meeting the Risen Christ, but both are equally parts of the paschal experience. The notes in *Lent, Holy Week, Easter* argue that, if at night, the celebration should be as late as possible, preferably after midnight. There is an appeal about 'getting the right day', but it is fairly artificial, and the important thing is that it should be dark by the end of the 'Vigil' part of the service before the paschal candle is lit. For good pastoral reasons, a parish may often find 9 o'clock on Saturday night a good time to introduce the Easter liturgy - people will often come then in a way that they will not at midnight or dawn - even if, once it is established and popular, it can be moved to one of these 'better' times.

Where Saturday evening and night and Sunday dawn are all impossible, this liturgy, omitting only the Vigil, can be used mid-morning on Easter Day, with the Service of Light (though admittedly not in darkness) and the liturgies of both baptism and Eucharist. For, at whatever hour it is celebrated, the most important factor is that it is at a time when the people will come. The idea of the 'Easter ceremonies' as an esoteric experience for a faithful few, enjoyed by those but quite outside the experience of most churchpeople, must give way to a liturgy for Easter that is at the heart of the spirituality of *all* the faithful. Having the people there is the first priority, maintaining the unity of the rite is the second. Celebrating it at the 'right' hour comes very much in third place.

All the services for Holy Week and Easter have a number of variations in them, but no other has two so fundamentally different alternative structures. In planning the service it is important to be clear from the start which is to be followed. Is the service to begin dramatically with the Service of Light and then settle down into a vigil of Old Testament material, giving way, after the *Gloria*, to the New Testament? That is the more traditional way, and the way in the Roman Missal, and the way many are familiar with. Or is it to begin with the vigil readings with silence in the dark, possibly ending with a passion reading, and then, having traced the story of our redemption to that point, begin the Easter celebrations with the Service of Light leading straight into the *Gloria*, Easter collect and New Testament lections? This has historic precedent, though more rarely, is novel for most, but is probably dramatically and psychologically more satisfying. *Lent, Holy Week, Easter* 'weights' the material in favour of this latter presentation, and, in what follows here, this second order will be assumed, though obviously there remains a case, other than simply tradition, for the Service of Light before the Vigil.

Before looking at the service stage by stage, two further points are worth noting.

The first is the name of the service. The 'Easter Ceremonies' immediately focuses the emphasis wrongly and suggests something peripheral. The 'Easter Vigil' has become common, and has seemed appropriate where the service has been entirely in the dark. But it seems more helpful now to restrict that term to the stage within the service where watching and waiting, aided by scripture reading, prepare the faithful for Easter. 'The Easter Liturgy' is what *Lent, Holy Week, Easter* calls it and, in many places, that would be suitable. But the word 'liturgy' is still not common parlance in the Church and would put some off. 'The Easter Celebration' would often be the happiest choice.

The second is simply to emphasize what was said in Chapter Two about the full use of the church building. Here is a service in which a quite small congregation in a vast church might nevertheless fill it and appreciate it as they move around it during the liturgy – the Vigil in the nave, the baptismal liturgy at the font, the Eucharist in the chancel. Let the people move!

The Vigil (sections 1 and 2) is the first stage of the Easter Liturgy. It may be a symbolic vigil of perhaps just three readings, with psalm or other oral response, silence and collect after each, the total lasting only twenty minutes or so. For such a vigil the congregation will all be expected to have arrived before it begins. Or it may be a much longer vigil, as many hours as are wanted, if desired right through the night, with not only readings, psalms and collects, but sermons, drama, films even, and people arriving at various points throughout. Or it may be somewhere between these two extremes, both in its length and in the formality of its liturgical style. The fundamental aim needs to be kept firmly in mind. It is an entering into the experience of Christ; as he awaits his vindication, so we watch and wait for the proclamation of the resurrection. It is also a devout recalling of our history as the people of God, from the creation through until the new creation that Easter will celebrate. In particular it sets before us, in certain stories, 'types' of the death-resurrection experience which illuminate our understanding of it, of which, of course, the Exodus event is the most striking.

The setting for the Vigil will usually be the darkened church. One light will be needed by which to read. Despite tenth century Jerusalem practice, a candle lit before the paschal candle is probably confusing, and therefore unhelpful, symbolism, and a single dim electric light that can later be switched off is probably best. (Those who advocate the Service of Light and the Vigil in the other order see this as the weakest point in the order we are following. Doing it *their* way, the paschal candle provides the light for the vigil readings!) Though there is a role for the president, introducing the Vigil (section 1) and probably saying the collects, this is only a semi-liturgical stage in the celebration, a sort of extended preparation; the president probably enters very informally, wears no vestments and is not attended by other ministers – they are seated 'in the congregation' but ready to slip out to vest when the Service of Light is near. There is a case for holding the Vigil in another building, for instance, especially if the people are to be outside for the lighting of the candle before following it into the church.

The choice of material for the Vigil is left to local decision from the long and imaginative provision. Lay people will, naturally, be involved in these readings. The psalms may be said or sung, omitted altogether or replaced by hymns or other songs. The Negro spiritual 'When Israel was in Egypt's land, let my people go' may, for instance, seem as powerful a response to the Exodus 14 reading as the canticle *Cantemus Domino*. The only readings that are particularly urged for inclusion are the creation story in Genesis 1 and the flight from Egypt in Exodus 14. (Where a vigil is not kept, this latter passage becomes the strongest candidate as an Old Testament reading within the Eucharist itself, for without the Exodus imagery clear in the minds of the worshippers a lot of material at Easter, not least in hymns, will be lost on them.)

> The Lamb's high banquet called to share
> Arrayed in garments white and fair,
> The Red Sea past, we fain would sing
> To Jesus our triumphant King.

For most the provision of the passion narrative within the Vigil will be novel. It is, of course, a return to the primitive unitive paschal celebration, where death and resurrection belong together. Whether it can work when the people have already heard two full passion gospels, on Palm Sunday and Good Friday, must be a matter for experiment; it could mean an overuse of passion material. Whether it, or some other, be the last of the vigil readings, it should give way to a longer silence in complete darkness, marked, if the Vigil has done its work well, by expectancy and anticipation.

The Service of Light now follows (sections 3 to 17). The main text and rubrics make no reference to fire, but the introductory essay notes and commends the tradition of lighting the candle from 'the new fire', which may be a small fire in the church porch, around which the ministers stand, or a great bonfire (with

107

branches from Palm Sunday?), around which all the congregation, coming out of the church, may gather. In the silence that precedes the Service of Light, the ministers vest in white or gold vestments and go to the fire with the unlighted candle. The fire is not lit as part of the liturgy. Those who are looking after it should have it burning when the ministers arrive at it. The members of the congregation, if they do not all go outside around the fire, turn to face it. If there is a danger that they will not *hear* what is outside or in the porch, a microphone is desirable. Of the words provided at section 5, the first (6) is most obviously appropriate where there is a fire, the second (7) may accompany the tracing on the candle of a cross, the alpha and omega letters and the year, and the third (8) is suitable if the five 'nails' are inserted to represent the wounds of Christ. The president then lights the candle from fire or taper as he says, 'May the light of Christ, rising in glory, banish all darkness from our hearts and minds.'

The procession now enters the church. The paschal candle, borne by the president, or by another minister (a deacon, by tradition, if one is present), is at the *head* of the procession; even a processional cross goes behind. The rubric permits the gospel at this early point. It provides the biblical witness to what is to be proclaimed. If read at this point, at the door, by the light of the paschal candle, it is read without the usual announcements and acclamations – all that is to follow is an extended acclamation and response. Many however will prefer the more gradual permeation of the Easter message through the next sections of the liturgy until it is spelt out, and the story reheard, in the gospel at the traditional point later in the service.

The procession moves through the church. As it goes, all light their individual candles either directly from it or, when numbers are great, by light passed from one to another, until the whole church is a mass of candle light. At three points during the procession the paschal candle bearer says or sings 'The light of Christ' with the people's response 'Thanks be to God'. The tradition, when it is sung, is that it goes up a tone each time. This procession takes time and the lighting of candles slows it down. Some delay is inevitable and can heighten expectancy.

But, if it lasts too long, momentum is lost. To avoid this, careful planning is needed to ensure that all candles are lit as speedily and efficiently as possible.

The procession comes to the candle stand. This need not necessarily be at the altar. There is a stronger argument for it being at the lectern, or at least that a temporary lectern be placed by it tonight for the *Exultet* and remaining reading(s). But what is important is that it should be in a public and prominent place, clearly visible and accessible. At section 16, as the candle is placed on its stand, the words 'Alleluia. Christ is risen.', with the response 'He is risen indeed. Alleluia.' may be used. An earlier note suggests that this can be repeated, three times perhaps, with an increase in volume each time, so that it begins with a whisper and ends with a shout! This is the congregation's first opportunity to respond to what is being proclaimed. The third exchange might lead into a fanfare on trumpet or organ.

The *Exultet* (section 17) follows. It is an ancient and beautiful Easter song and, by tradition, the deacon sings it. The chant for it is very attractive and the *Exultet*, sung well, very moving. But not every church has anyone equipped to sing a long solo passage in this style, and indeed not every congregation will respond to its musical form, however beautifully rendered. It may be said, rather than sung, but this could be somewhat lame. Yet its omission altogether would be a loss. In two ways a spoken, rather than sung, presentation of it can be made more effective. First, it can be made a quieter element between two great musical bursts of praise: a fanfare already mentioned beforehand, and a vibrant sung congregational *Gloria* immediately after. Second, it can be made more congregational, with some stanzas printed for all to say, so that it takes on a more responsorial character.

Gloria in Excelsis (secton 19) provides the transition to the usual eucharistic shape and the moment to turn on all the lights. There is a tradition of making this a very dramatic moment, with a great burst on the organ (all the more dramatic if it has been silent to this point), the church bell(s) ringing out, together with handbells and other musical sounds, as the church is filled with light, as a grand build up to the *Gloria*. The rubric allows a hymn in place of the *Gloria*, and, in places where the *Gloria* is usually said rather than sung, a hymn will be preferable as a great congregational finale to what has gone before. Almost inevitably 'Jesus Christ is risen today' commends itself at this point.

The president then says the collect (section 20) after which all still holding their candles sit for the epistle reading, Paul's words to the Romans on the paschal nature of baptism. What is to happen after the epistle will depend on the previous decision about the position of the gospel. If it has already been read at the door, the service now moves to the sermon. Although this may seem strange within a eucharistic context, a baptismal reading, leading into an address to link it with the Liturgy of Initiation, which is to follow immediately, is a logical and satisfactory progression. On the other hand, if the gospel is to come at this later point, the psalm (section 22), with its *alleluia* response, or, alternatively, an *alleluia* hymn, links epistle with gospel in the normal way. Before the sermon the people's candles are extinguished – perhaps at the invitation of the preacher who first invites the people to hold the candles high for a further exchange of the Easter greeting.

The Liturgy of Initiation, which follows the sermon, is at least a Renewal of Baptismal vows (section 26) with a concluding collect, but it may include the celebration of both baptism and confirmation, where this is possible and pastorally desirable. The Renewal of Vows, without a baptism to put the congregation in mind of their own baptism, is slightly lame, and, when there is no baptism, a marvellous teaching occasion, in which the relationship between the paschal mystery and Christian baptism is plain to see, is lost. So, without quite seeking out candidates, the priest does well to keep in mind possible candidates for this occasion. Where there cannot be the celebration of a baptism, there are ways in which the Renewal of Vows can be given a stronger emphasis. The first is a procession to the font, so that all may turn to face it as the focus for this part of the liturgy. The second is the blessing of the water before the vows are made. A note allows this and the text is provided in an appendix.

The third, which is not within the notes or rubrics, is to sprinkle the people with the baptismal water in response to the renewal of their vows. Many who would not normally advocate the sprinkling of holy water might see in this particular action a powerful symbolism. The fourth is to relight the candles for the renewal of vows, though this could detract from the water symbolism at this point.

Although the transition from the vows to the greeting of Peace is a natural one, many will be concerned at the omission of the prayers of intercession. Conscious of this problem, *Lent, Holy Week, Easter* has provided for each of the special services of this week a short, concise and seasonal form of intercession, that for this occasion being found, not within the service itself, but in 'Prayers for use in Eastertide'.

The liturgy continues with the Peace and thereafter follows the Rite A order, with the addition of many *alleluias* and other Easter responses. That before communion, from the Rite A appendix, deserves a place in every Eucharist through Eastertide and is soon memorized, and the Easter form of the Dismissal should also be retained throughout the season. Where the Dismissal is sung, local initiative will often have to adapt existing texts, so that there may be a glorious and joyful ending both at the Easter liturgy itself and throughout the season. 'The Liturgy of the Eucharist' within the total service of Easter night and day needs a pace and liveliness to it if there is not to be a sense of anticlimax where the special material gives way to the familiar. That is why the repetitive exclamatory Easter greetings and responses are so helpful. They help to keep the special atmosphere so that the climax really is where it should be - in sacramental reunion with the Risen Lord. If there are bells, though they should have been silent before the service, they can ring out now to usher in the great fifty days.

Although an Easter celebration without Holy Communion runs contrary to the recommendations of the book, provision is made for such a service. It is brought to a conclusion after the Renewal of Vows or the Intercession by other possible prayers, a hymn and the Easter blessing. Suitable prayers include the Thanksgiving for the Resurrection in 'Prayers for Use in

Eastertide' and a special note indicates that the final hymn could be *Gloria in excelsis*, held over from its earlier position, to provide a non-eucharistic climax to the liturgy. (It must be noted that it occupies a crucial climactic position at section 19 after the *Exultet* and its removal from there could be mistaken.)

The Easter Season

The section of *Lent, Holy Week, Easter* entitled 'The Easter Season' does not include the text of any service, and so some may pass over it without much care. This would be a grave error. For the rediscovery of the Great Fifty Days until Pentecost would be a great enrichment of Church liturgy and life. The careful choice of Easter hymnody, the repeated use of the *alleluia*, the special paschal greeting, invitation to communion and dismissal, the lighting of the paschal candle, throughout the season, together with a general awareness of the distinctiveness and unity of this time (as much as of Lent that precedes it) would all greatly enhance the celebration of the period until Pentecost evening. A careful reading and heeding of these paragraphs of *Lent, Holy Week, Easter* is much to be recommended.

Select Bibliography

Texts

Liturgies pascales à Taizé. Presses de Taizé 1971.
The Holy Week liturgy of the Taizé Community.

The Book of Common Prayer (Seabury, New York 1979), pp. 264-95.
The Lent, Holy Week and Easter liturgy of the Episcopal Church of the USA.

Lord, By Your Cross and Resurrection: Celebrating Holy Week. St Thomas More Centre for Pastoral Liturgy 1979.
Roman Catholic Holy Week Liturgy. (In this text, the Joint Liturgical Group structure for the Vigil is adopted.)

Gray, Donald, ed., *Holy Week Services* (revised and expanded). SPCK 1983[2].
The recent revision of services produced by the Joint Liturgical Group.

Studies

Berger, R. and Hollerweger, H., (ed.), *Celebrating the Easter Vigil.* New York, Pueblo, 1983.
Historical background with practical suggestions about the homily, as well as domestic prayers.

Crichton, J.D., *The Liturgy of Holy Week.* Veritas/Fowler Wright, 1983.
A brief historical survey, concentrating on the new Roman Catholic rites.

Perham, Michael, *Liturgy Pastoral and Parochial* (SPCK 1984), pp. 170-202.
Suggestions on how to implement traditional and experimental services for Lent, Holy Week, Easter, and Pentecost.

SELECT BIBLIOGRAPHY

Schmidt, Hermann, *Hebdomada Sancta* I-II. Rome, Herder, 1956-7.
Detailed historical commentary on the historical development of the main Western medieval rites. (In Latin.)

Stevenson, Kenneth W., 'On Keeping Holy Week' (*Theology* no. 727, January 1986), pp. 32-8.
Short analysis of paschal pieties and the new Church of England services.

Stevenson, Kenneth W., 'The Ceremonies of Light - Their Shape and Function in the Paschal Vigil Liturgy' (*Ephemerides Liturgicae* 99, 1985), pp. 170-85.
Detailed historical and theological analysis of the shape of the Easter Vigil.

Taft, Robert F., 'Historicism Revisited', in Taft, Robert F., *Beyond East and West: Problems in Liturgical Understanding* (Washington, Pastoral Press, 1984), pp. 15-30.
Review of the concept of 'historicism' before and after the fourth century.

Talley, Thomas J., *The Origins of the Liturgical Year*. New York, Pueblo, 1986.
The most important study of the development of the Church's year published recently.

Wilkinson, John, *Egeria's Travels*. SPCK 1971[1] and Aris and Phillips/Ariel Publishing House, 1981[2] (this latter a revised and expanded edition).
An edition of the diary of Egeria, the fourth century nun who visited Jerusalem in the latter part of the fourth century and who made careful notes on the liturgy there.